HBR's 10 Must Reads

UPDATED & EXPANDED

Managing People

HBR's 10 Must Reads

HBR's 10 Must Reads are definitive collections of classic ideas, practical advice, and essential thinking from the pages of *Harvard Business Review*. Exploring topics like disruptive innovation, emotional intelligence, and new technology in our ever-evolving world, these books empower any leader to make bold decisions and inspire others.

TITLES INCLUDE:

- HBR's 10 Must Reads for New Managers
- HBR's 10 Must Reads on AI
- HBR's 10 Must Reads on Building a Great Culture
- HBR's 10 Must Reads on Change Management
- HBR's 10 Must Reads on Communication
- HBR's 10 Must Reads on Data Strategy
- HBR's 10 Must Reads on Decision-Making
- HBR's 10 Must Reads on Design Thinking
- HBR's 10 Must Reads on Digital Transformation
- HBR's 10 Must Reads on Emotional Intelligence
- HBR's 10 Must Reads on High Performance
- HBR's 10 Must Reads on Innovation
- HBR's 10 Must Reads on Leadership
- HBR's 10 Must Reads on Leading Winning Teams
- HBR's 10 Must Reads on Managing People
- HBR's 10 Must Reads on Managing Yourself
- HBR's 10 Must Reads on Marketing
- HBR's 10 Must Reads on Mental Toughness
- HBR's 10 Must Reads on Strategy
- HBR's 10 Must Reads on Women and Leadership
- HBR's 10 Must Reads Boxed Set (6 Books)
- HBR's 10 Must Reads Ultimate Boxed Set (14 Books)

For a full list, visit hbr.org/mustreads.

# HBR's 10 Must Reads

UPDATED & EXPANDED

Managing People

Harvard Business Review Press
Boston, Massachusetts

HBR Press Quantity Sales Discounts

Harvard Business Review Press titles are available at significant quantity discounts when purchased in bulk for client gifts, sales promotions, and premiums. Special editions, including books with corporate logos, customized covers, and letters from the company or CEO printed in the front matter, as well as excerpts of existing books, can also be created in large quantities for special needs. For details and discount information for both print and ebook formats, contact booksales@harvardbusiness.org, tel. 800-988-0886, or www.hbr.org/bulksales.

Copyright 2025 Harvard Business School Publishing Corporation

All rights reserved

Printed in the United States of America

10 9 8 7 6 5 4 3 2 1

No part of this publication may be reproduced, stored in or introduced into a retrieval system, or transmitted, in any form, or by any means (electronic, mechanical, photocopying, recording, or otherwise), without the prior permission of the publisher. Requests for permission should be directed to permissions@harvardbusiness.org, or mailed to Permissions, Harvard Business School Publishing, 60 Harvard Way, Boston, Massachusetts 02163.

The web addresses referenced in this book were live and correct at the time of the book's publication but may be subject to change.

Cataloging-in-Publication data is forthcoming.

The paper used in this publication meets the requirements of the American National Standard for Permanence of Paper for Publications and Documents in Libraries and Archives Z39.48-1992.

ISBN: 979-8-89279-170-0
eISBN: 979-8-89279-171-7

Contents

1. Leadership That Gets Results — 1
You should have more than one style in your repertoire.

by **Daniel Goleman**

2. The Power of Small Wins — 33
Nothing motivates people like making progress in meaningful work.

by **Teresa M. Amabile and Steven J. Kramer**

3. The Leader as Coach — 57
Unleash innovation, energy, and commitment.

by **Herminia Ibarra and Anne Scoular**

QUICK READ

Superbosses Aren't Afraid to Delegate Their Biggest Decisions — 75
You don't need a cape. You need trust.

by **Sydney Finkelstein**

4. The Set-Up-to-Fail Syndrome — 81
Dealing with an underperformer? Maybe you're the problem.

by **Jean-François Manzoni and Jean-Louis Barsoux**

5 The Overcommitted Organization 109
Avoid the pitfalls of sharing talented people across teams.

by Mark Mortensen and Heidi K. Gardner

6 Global Teams That Work 129
Help people connect across distance and difference.

by Tsedal Neeley

QUICK READ

Four Types of Team Conflict—and How to Resolve Them 147
Be proactive and turn disagreements into success stories.

by Randall S. Peterson, Priti Pradhan Shah, Amanda J. Ferguson, and Stephen L. Jones

7 Why Employees Quit 157
And the key factors that compel them to stay.

by Ethan Bernstein, Michael B. Horn, and Bob Moesta

8 The Feedback Fallacy 181
Real growth requires more than praise and criticism.

by Marcus Buckingham and Ashley Goodall

> **QUICK READ**
>
> ### To Excel, Diverse Teams Need Psychological Safety 199
> People from different backgrounds clash without it.
>
> **by Henrik Bresman and Amy C. Edmondson**

9. Managers Can't Do It All 207
If you're struggling to keep up, you're not alone.

by Diane Gherson and Lynda Gratton

10. Are You a Good Boss—or a Great One? 223
The best managers never stop learning.

by Linda A. Hill and Kent Lineback

Discussion Guide	241
Notes	247
About the Contributors	249
Index	255

HBR's 10 Must Reads

UPDATED & EXPANDED

Managing People

Leadership That Gets Results

by Daniel Goleman

Ask any group of businesspeople the question "What do effective leaders do?" and you'll hear a sweep of answers. Leaders set strategy; they motivate; they create a mission; they build a culture. Then ask "What should leaders do?" If the group is seasoned, you'll likely hear one response: The leader's singular job is to get results.

But how? The mystery of what leaders can and ought to do in order to spark the best performance from their people is age-old. In recent years, that mystery has spawned an entire cottage industry: literally thousands of "leadership experts" have made careers of testing and coaching executives, all in pursuit of creating businesspeople who can turn bold objectives—be they strategic, financial, organizational, or all three—into reality.

Editor's Note: Daniel Goleman consults with Hay/McBer on leadership development.

Still, effective leadership eludes many people and organizations. One reason is that until recently, virtually no quantitative research has demonstrated which precise leadership behaviors yield positive results. Leadership experts proffer advice based on inference, experience, and instinct. Sometimes that advice is right on target; sometimes it's not.

But new research by the consulting firm Hay/McBer, which draws on a random sample of 3,871 executives selected from a database of more than 20,000 executives worldwide, takes much of the mystery out of effective leadership. The research found six distinct leadership styles, each springing from different components of emotional intelligence. The styles, taken individually, appear to have a direct and unique impact on the working atmosphere of a company, division, or team, and in turn, on its financial performance. And perhaps most important, the research indicates that leaders with the best results do not rely on only one leadership style; they use most of them in a given week—seamlessly and in different measure—depending on the business situation. Imagine the styles, then, as the array of clubs in a golf pro's bag. Over the course of a game, the pro picks and chooses clubs based on the demands of the shot. Sometimes he has to ponder his selection, but usually it is automatic. The pro senses the challenge ahead, swiftly pulls out the right tool, and elegantly puts it to work. That's how high-impact leaders operate, too.

What are the six styles of leadership? None will shock workplace veterans. Indeed, each style, by name and brief description alone, will likely resonate with anyone who leads, is led, or as is the case with most of us, does both. Coercive leaders demand immediate compliance. Authoritative leaders mobilize people toward a vision. Affiliative leaders create emotional bonds and

Idea in Brief

Many managers mistakenly assume that leadership style is a function of personality rather than strategic choice. Instead of choosing the one style that suits their temperament, they should ask which style best addresses the demands of a particular situation.

Research has shown that the most successful leaders have strengths in the following emotional intelligence competencies: self-awareness, self-regulation, motivation, empathy, and social skill. There are six basic styles of leadership; each makes use of the key components of emotional intelligence in different combinations. The best leaders don't know just one style of leadership—they're skilled at several, and have the flexibility to switch between styles as the circumstances dictate.

harmony. Democratic leaders build consensus through participation. Pacesetting leaders expect excellence and self-direction. And coaching leaders develop people for the future.

Close your eyes and you can surely imagine a colleague who uses any one of these styles. You most likely use at least one yourself. What is new in this research, then, is its implications for action. First, it offers a fine-grained understanding of how different leadership styles affect performance and results. Second, it offers clear guidance on when a manager should switch between them. It also strongly suggests that switching flexibly is well advised. New, too, is the research's finding that each leadership style springs from different components of emotional intelligence.

Measuring Leadership's Impact

It has been more than a decade since research first linked aspects of emotional intelligence to business results. The late David McClelland, a noted Harvard University psychologist,

Emotional Intelligence: A Primer

Emotional intelligence—the ability to manage ourselves and our relationships effectively—consists of four fundamental capabilities: self-awareness, self-management, social awareness, and social skill. Each capability, in turn, is composed of specific sets of competencies. Below is a list of the capabilities and their corresponding traits.

Self-Awareness

- Emotional self-awareness: the ability to read and understand your emotions as well as recognize their impact on work performance, relationships, and the like

- Accurate self-assessment: a realistic evaluation of your strengths and limitations

- Self-confidence: a strong and positive sense of self-worth

Self-Management

- Self-control: the ability to keep disruptive emotions and impulses under control

- Trustworthiness: a consistent display of honesty and integrity

- Conscientiousness: the ability to manage yourself and your responsibilities

- Adaptability: skill at adjusting to changing situations and overcoming obstacles

- Achievement orientation: the drive to meet an internal standard of excellence

- Initiative: a readiness to seize opportunities

Social Awareness

- Empathy: skill at sensing other people's emotions, understanding their perspective, and taking an active interest in their concerns
- Organizational awareness: the ability to read the currents of organizational life, build decision networks, and navigate politics
- Service orientation: the ability to recognize and meet customers' needs

Social Skill

- Visionary leadership: the ability to take charge and inspire with a compelling vision
- Influence: the ability to wield a range of persuasive tactics
- Developing others: the propensity to bolster the abilities of others through feedback and guidance
- Communication: skill at listening and at sending clear, convincing, and well-tuned messages
- Change catalyst: proficiency in initiating new ideas and leading people in a new direction
- Conflict management: the ability to de-escalate disagreements and orchestrate resolutions
- Building bonds: proficiency at cultivating and maintaining a web of relationships
- Teamwork and collaboration: competence at promoting cooperation and building teams

found that leaders with strengths in a critical mass of six or more emotional intelligence competencies were far more effective than peers who lacked such strengths. For instance, when he analyzed the performance of division heads at a global food and beverage company, he found that among leaders with this critical mass of competence, 87% placed in the top third for annual salary bonuses based on their business performance. More telling, their divisions on average outperformed yearly revenue targets by 15% to 20%. Those executives who lacked emotional intelligence were rarely rated as outstanding in their annual performance reviews, and their divisions underperformed by an average of almost 20%.

Our research set out to gain a more molecular view of the links among leadership and emotional intelligence, and climate and performance. A team of McClelland's colleagues headed by Mary Fontaine and Ruth Jacobs from Hay/McBer studied data about or observed thousands of executives, noting specific behaviors and their impact on climate. How did each individual motivate direct reports? Manage change initiatives? Handle crises? It was in a later phase of the research that we identified which emotional intelligence capabilities drive the six leadership styles. How does he rate in terms of self-control and social skill? Does a leader show high or low levels of empathy?

The team tested each executive's immediate sphere of influence for its climate. "Climate" is not an amorphous term. First defined by psychologists George Litwin and Richard Stringer and later refined by McClelland and his colleagues, it refers to six key factors that influence an organization's working environment: its flexibility—that is, how free employees feel to innovate unencumbered by red tape; their sense of responsibility to the organization; the level of standards that people set; the sense of

Getting Molecular: The Impact of Leadership Styles on Drivers of Climate

Our research investigated how each leadership style affected the six drivers of climate, or working atmosphere. The figures below show the correlation between each leadership style and each aspect of climate. So, for instance, if we look at the climate driver of flexibility, we see that the coercive style has a -.28 correlation while the democratic style has a .28 correlation, equally strong in the opposite direction. Focusing on the authoritative leadership style, we find that it has a .54 correlation with rewards—strongly positive—and a .21 correlation with responsibility—positive, but not as strong. In other words, the style's correlation with rewards was more than twice that with responsibility.

According to the data, the authoritative leadership style has the most positive effect on climate, but three others—affiliative, democratic, and coaching—follow close behind. That said, the research indicates that no style should be relied on exclusively, and all have at least short-term uses.

	Coercive	Authoritative	Affiliative	Democratic	Pacesetting	Coaching
Flexibility	-.28	.32	.27	.28	-.07	.17
Responsibility	-.37	.21	.16	.23	.04	.08
Standards	.02	.38	.31	.22	-.27	.39
Rewards	-.18	.54	.48	.42	-.29	.43
Clarity	-.11	.44	.37	.35	-.28	.38
Commitment	-.13	.35	.34	.26	-.20	.27
Overall impact on climate	-.26	.54	.46	.43	-.25	.42

accuracy about performance feedback and aptness of rewards; the clarity people have about mission and values; and finally, the level of commitment to a common purpose.

We found that all six leadership styles have a measurable effect on each aspect of climate. (For details, see the sidebar "Getting Molecular: The Impact of Leadership Styles on Drivers of Climate.") Further, when we looked at the impact of climate on financial results—such as return on sales, revenue growth, efficiency, and profitability—we found a direct correlation between the two. Leaders who used styles that positively affected the climate had decidedly better financial results than those who did not. That is not to say that organizational climate is the only driver of performance. Economic conditions and competitive dynamics matter enormously. But our analysis strongly suggests that climate accounts for nearly a third of results. And that's simply too much of an impact to ignore.

The Styles in Detail

Executives use six leadership styles, but only four of the six consistently have a positive effect on climate and results. Let's look then at each style of leadership in detail. (For a summary of the material that follows, see the chart "The six leadership styles at a glance.")

The coercive style

The computer company was in crisis mode—its sales and profits were falling, its stock was losing value precipitously, and its shareholders were in an uproar. The board brought in a new CEO with a reputation as a turnaround artist. He set to work chopping jobs, selling off divisions, and making the tough decisions that should have been executed years before. The company was saved, at least in the short-term.

From the start, though, the CEO created a reign of terror, bullying and demeaning his executives, roaring his displeasure at the slightest misstep. The company's top echelons were decimated not just by his erratic firings but also by defections. The CEO's direct reports, frightened by his tendency to blame the bearer of bad news, stopped bringing him any news at all. Morale was at an all-time low—a fact reflected in another downturn in the business after the short-term recovery. The CEO was eventually fired by the board of directors.

It's easy to understand why of all the leadership styles, the coercive one is the least effective in most situations. Consider what the style does to an organization's climate. Flexibility is the hardest hit. The leader's extreme top-down decision-making kills new ideas on the vine. People feel so disrespected that they think, "I won't even bring my ideas up—they'll only be shot down." Likewise, people's sense of responsibility evaporates: unable to act on their own initiative, they lose their sense of ownership and feel little accountability for their performance. Some become so resentful they adopt the attitude, "I'm not going to help this bastard."

Coercive leadership also has a damaging effect on the rewards system. Most high-performing workers are motivated by more than money—they seek the satisfaction of work well done. The coercive style erodes such pride. And finally, the style undermines one of the leader's prime tools—motivating people by showing them how their job fits into a grand, shared mission. Such a loss, measured in terms of diminished clarity and commitment, leaves people alienated from their own jobs, wondering, "How does any of this matter?"

The six leadership styles at a glance

Our research found that leaders use six styles, each springing from different components of emotional intelligence. Here is a summary of the styles, their origin, when they work best, and their impact on an organization's climate and thus its performance.

	Coercive	Authoritative
The leader's modus operandi	Demands immediate compliance	Mobilizes people toward a vision
The style in a phrase	"Do what I tell you."	"Come with me."
Underlying emotional intelligence competencies	Drive to achieve, initiative, self-control	Self-confidence, empathy, change catalyst
When the style works best	In a crisis, to kick-start a turnaround, or with problem employees	When changes require a new vision, or when a clear direction is needed
Overall impact on climate	Negative	Most strongly positive

Given the impact of the coercive style, you might assume it should never be applied. Our research, however, uncovered a few occasions when it worked masterfully. Take the case of a division president who was brought in to change the direction of a food company that was losing money. His first act was to have the executive conference room demolished. To him, the room—with its long marble table that looked like "the deck of the Starship *Enterprise*"—symbolized the tradition-bound formality that was paralyzing the company. The destruction of the room, and the subsequent move to a smaller, more informal setting, sent a message no one could miss, and the division's culture changed quickly in its wake.

That said, the coercive style should be used only with extreme caution and in the few situations when it is absolutely imperative,

Affiliative	Democratic	Pacesetting	Coaching
Creates harmony and builds emotional bonds	Forges consensus through participation	Sets high standards for performance	Develops people for the future
"People come first."	"What do you think?"	"Do as I do, now."	"Try this."
Empathy, building relationships, communication	Collaboration, team leadership, communication	Conscientiousness, drive to achieve, initiative	Developing others, empathy, self-awareness
To heal rifts in a team or to motivate people during stressful circumstances	To build buy-in or consensus, or to get input from valuable employees	To get quick results from a highly motivated and competent team	To help an employee improve performance or develop long-term strengths
Positive	Positive	Negative	Positive

such as during a turnaround or when a hostile takeover is looming. In those cases, the coercive style can break failed business habits and shock people into new ways of working. It is always appropriate during a genuine emergency, like in the aftermath of an earthquake or a fire. And it can work with problem employees with whom all else has failed. But if a leader relies solely on this style or continues to use it once the emergency passes, the long-term impact of his insensitivity to the morale and feelings of those he leads will be ruinous.

The authoritative style

Tom was the vice president of marketing at a floundering national restaurant chain that specialized in pizza. Needless to say, the company's poor performance troubled the senior managers, but they were at a loss for what to do. Every Monday, they met to review recent sales, struggling to come up with fixes. To Tom, the approach didn't make sense. "We were always trying to figure out why our sales were down last week. We had the whole company looking backward instead of figuring out what we had to do tomorrow."

Tom saw an opportunity to change people's way of thinking at an off-site strategy meeting. There, the conversation began with stale truisms: the company had to drive up shareholder wealth and increase return on assets. Tom believed those concepts didn't have the power to inspire a restaurant manager to be innovative or to do better than a good-enough job.

So Tom made a bold move. In the middle of a meeting, he made an impassioned plea for his colleagues to think from the customer's perspective. Customers want convenience, he said. The company was not in the restaurant business, it was in the business of distributing high-quality, convenient-to-get pizza. That notion—and nothing else—should drive everything the company did.

With his vibrant enthusiasm and clear vision—the hallmarks of the authoritative style—Tom filled a leadership vacuum at the company. Indeed, his concept became the core of the new mission statement. But this conceptual breakthrough was just the beginning. Tom made sure that the mission statement was built into the company's strategic planning process as the designated driver of growth. And he ensured that the vision was articulated so that local restaurant managers understood they were the key to the company's success and were free to find new ways to distribute pizza.

Changes came quickly. Within weeks, many local managers started guaranteeing fast, new delivery times. Even better, they started to act like entrepreneurs, finding ingenious locations to open new branches: kiosks on busy street corners and in bus and train stations, even from carts in airports and hotel lobbies.

Tom's success was no fluke. Our research indicates that of the six leadership styles, the authoritative one is most effective, driving up every aspect of climate. Take clarity. The authoritative leader is a visionary; he motivates people by making clear to them how their work fits into a larger vision for the organization. People who work for such leaders understand that what they do matters and why. Authoritative leadership also maximizes commitment to the organization's goals and strategy. By framing the individual tasks within a grand vision, the authoritative leader defines standards that revolve around that vision. When he gives performance feedback—whether positive or negative—the singular criterion is whether or not that performance furthers the vision. The standards for success are clear to all, as are the rewards. Finally, consider the style's impact on flexibility. An authoritative leader states the end but generally gives people plenty of leeway to devise their own means. Authoritative leaders give people the freedom to innovate, experiment, and take calculated risks.

Because of its positive impact, the authoritative style works well in almost any business situation. But it is particularly effective when a business is adrift. An authoritative leader charts a new course and sells his people on a fresh long-term vision.

The authoritative style, powerful though it may be, will not work in every situation. The approach fails, for instance, when a leader is working with a team of experts or peers who are more experienced than he is; they may see the leader as pompous or out-of-touch. Another limitation: if a manager trying to be authoritative becomes overbearing, he can undermine the egalitarian spirit of an effective team. Yet even with such caveats, leaders would be wise to grab for the authoritative "club" more often than not. It may not guarantee a hole in one, but it certainly helps with the long drive.

The affiliative style

If the coercive leader demands, "Do what I say," and the authoritative urges, "Come with me," the affiliative leader says, "People come first." This leadership style revolves around people—its proponents value individuals and their emotions more than tasks and goals. The affiliative leader strives to keep employees happy and to create harmony among them. He manages by building strong emotional bonds and then reaping the benefits of such an approach, namely fierce loyalty. The style also has a markedly positive effect on communication. People who like one another a lot talk a lot. They share ideas; they share inspiration. And the style drives up flexibility; friends trust one another, allowing habitual innovation and risk taking. Flexibility also rises because the affiliative leader, like a parent who adjusts household rules for a maturing adolescent, doesn't impose unnecessary strictures on how employees get their work done. They give people the freedom to do their job in the way they think is most effective.

As for a sense of recognition and reward for work well done, the affiliative leader offers ample positive feedback. Such feedback has special potency in the workplace because it is all too rare: outside of an annual review, most people usually get no feedback on their day-to-day efforts—or only negative feedback. That makes the affiliative leader's positive words all the more motivating. Finally, affiliative leaders are masters at building a sense of belonging. They are, for instance, likely to take their direct reports out for a meal or a drink, one-on-one, to see how they're doing. They will bring in a cake to celebrate a group accomplishment. They are natural relationship builders.

Joe Torre, the heart and soul of the New York Yankees, is a classic affiliative leader. During the 1999 World Series, Torre tended ably to the psyches of his players as they endured the emotional pressure cooker of a pennant race. All season long, he made a special point to praise Scott Brosius, whose father had died during the season, for staying committed even as he mourned. At the celebration party after the team's final game, Torre specifically sought out right fielder Paul O'Neill. Although he had received the news of his father's death that morning, O'Neill chose to play in the decisive game—and he burst into tears the moment it ended. Torre made a point of acknowledging O'Neill's personal struggle, calling him a "warrior." Torre also used the spotlight of the victory celebration to praise two players whose return the following year was threatened by contract disputes. In doing so, he sent a clear message to the team and to the club's owner that he valued the players immensely—too much to lose them.

Along with ministering to the emotions of his people, an affiliative leader may also tend to his own emotions openly. The year Torre's brother was near death awaiting a heart transplant, he shared his worries with his players. He also spoke candidly with the team about his treatment for prostate cancer.

The affiliative style's generally positive impact makes it a good all-weather approach, but leaders should employ it particularly when trying to build team harmony, increase morale, improve communication, or repair broken trust. For instance, one executive in our study was hired to replace a ruthless team leader. The former leader had taken credit for his employees' work and had attempted to pit them against one another. His efforts ultimately failed, but the team he left behind was suspicious and weary. The new executive managed to mend the situation by unstintingly showing emotional honesty and rebuilding ties. Several months in, her leadership had created a renewed sense of commitment and energy.

Despite its benefits, the affiliative style should not be used alone. Its exclusive focus on praise can allow poor performance to go uncorrected; employees may perceive that mediocrity is tolerated. And because affiliative leaders rarely offer constructive advice on how to improve, employees must figure out how to do so on their own. When people need clear directives to navigate through complex challenges, the affiliative style leaves them rudderless. Indeed, if overly relied on, this style can actually steer a group to failure. Perhaps that is why many affiliative leaders, including Torre, use this style in close conjunction with the authoritative style. Authoritative leaders state a vision, set standards, and let people know how their work is furthering the group's goals. Alternate that with the caring, nurturing approach of the affiliative leader, and you have a potent combination.

The democratic style

Sister Mary ran a Catholic school system in a large metropolitan area. One of the schools—the only private school in an impoverished neighborhood—had been losing money for years, and the archdiocese could no longer afford to keep it open. When Sister Mary eventually got the order to shut it down, she didn't just lock the doors. She called a meeting of all the teachers and staff at the school and explained to them the details of the financial crisis—the first time anyone working at the school had been included in the business side of the institution. She asked for their ideas on ways to keep the school open and on how to handle the closing, should it come to that. Sister Mary spent much of her time at the meeting just listening.

She did the same at later meetings for school parents and for the community and during a successive series of meetings for the school's teachers and staff. After two months of meetings, the consensus was clear: the school would have to close. A plan was made to transfer students to other schools in the Catholic system.

The final outcome was no different than if Sister Mary had gone ahead and closed the school the day she was told to. But by allowing the school's constituents to reach that decision collectively, Sister Mary received none of the backlash that would have accompanied such a move. People mourned the loss of the school, but they understood its inevitability. Virtually no one objected.

Compare that with the experiences of a priest in our research who headed another Catholic school. He, too, was told to shut it down. And he did—by fiat. The result was disastrous: parents filed lawsuits, teachers and parents picketed, and local newspapers ran editorials attacking his decision. It took a year to resolve the disputes before he could finally go ahead and close the school.

Sister Mary exemplifies the democratic style in action—and its benefits. By spending time getting people's ideas and buy-in, a leader builds trust, respect, and commitment. By letting workers themselves have a say in decisions that affect their goals and how they do their work, the democratic leader drives up flexibility and responsibility. And by listening to employees' concerns, the democratic leader learns what to do to keep morale high. Finally, because they have a say in setting their goals and the standards for evaluating success, people operating in a democratic system tend to be very realistic about what can and cannot be accomplished.

However, the democratic style has its drawbacks, which is why its impact on climate is not as high as some of the other styles.

One of its more exasperating consequences can be endless meetings where ideas are mulled over, consensus remains elusive, and the only visible result is scheduling more meetings. Some democratic leaders use the style to put off making crucial decisions, hoping that enough thrashing things out will eventually yield a blinding insight. In reality, their people end up feeling confused and leaderless. Such an approach can even escalate conflicts.

When does the style work best? This approach is ideal when a leader is himself uncertain about the best direction to take and needs ideas and guidance from able employees. And even if a leader has a strong vision, the democratic style works well to generate fresh ideas for executing that vision.

The democratic style, of course, makes much less sense when employees are not competent or informed enough to offer sound advice. And it almost goes without saying that building consensus is wrongheaded in times of crisis. Take the case of a CEO whose computer company was severely threatened by changes in the market. He always sought consensus about what to do. As competitors stole customers and customers' needs changed, he kept appointing committees to consider the situation. When the market made a sudden shift because of a new technology, the CEO froze in his tracks. The board replaced him before he could appoint yet another task force to consider the situation. The new CEO, while occasionally democratic and affiliative, relied heavily on the authoritative style, especially in his first months.

The pacesetting style

Like the coercive style, the pacesetting style has its place in the leader's repertory, but it should be used sparingly. That's not what we expected to find. After all, the hallmarks of the pacesetting style sound admirable. The leader sets extremely high performance standards and exemplifies them himself. He is obsessive about doing things better and faster, and he asks the same of everyone around him. He quickly pinpoints poor performers and demands more from them. If they don't rise to the occasion, he replaces them with people who can. You would think such an approach would improve results, but it doesn't.

In fact, the pacesetting style destroys climate. Many employees feel overwhelmed by the pacesetter's demands for excellence, and their morale drops. Guidelines for working may be clear in the leader's head, but she does not state them clearly; she expects people to know what to do and even thinks, "If I have to tell you, you're the wrong person for the job." Work becomes not a matter of doing one's best along a clear course so much as second-guessing what the leader wants. At the same time, people often feel that the pacesetter doesn't trust them to work in their own way or to take initiative. Flexibility and responsibility evaporate; work becomes so task focused and routinized it's boring.

As for rewards, the pacesetter either gives no feedback on how people are doing or jumps in to take over when he thinks they're lagging. And if the leader should leave, people feel directionless—they're so used to "the expert" setting the rules. Finally, commitment dwindles under the regime of a pacesetting leader because people have no sense of how their personal efforts fit into the big picture.

For an example of the pacesetting style, take the case of Sam, a biochemist in R&D at a large pharmaceutical company. Sam's superb technical expertise made him an early star: he was the one everyone turned to when they needed help. Soon he was promoted to head of a team developing a new product. The other scientists on the team were as competent and self-motivated as Sam; his métier as team leader became offering himself as a model of how to do first-class scientific work under tremendous deadline pressure, pitching in when needed. His team completed its task in record time.

But then came a new assignment: Sam was put in charge of R&D for his entire division. As his tasks expanded and he had to articulate a vision, coordinate projects, delegate responsibility, and help develop others, Sam began to slip. Not trusting that his subordinates were as capable as he was, he became a micromanager, obsessed with details and taking over for others when their performance slackened. Instead of trusting them to improve with guidance and development, Sam found himself working nights and weekends after stepping in to take over for the head of a floundering research team. Finally, his own boss suggested, to his relief, that he return to his old job as head of a product development team.

Although Sam faltered, the pacesetting style isn't always a disaster. The approach works well when all employees are self-motivated, highly competent, and need little direction or coordination—for example, it can work for leaders of highly skilled and self-motivated professionals, like R&D groups or legal teams. And, given a talented team to lead, pace-setting does exactly that: gets work done on time or even ahead of schedule. Yet like any leadership style, pacesetting should never be used by itself.

The coaching style

A product unit at a global computer company had seen sales plummet from twice as much as its competitors to only half as much. So Lawrence, the president of the manufacturing division, decided to close the unit and reassign its people and products.

Upon hearing the news, James, the head of the doomed unit, decided to go over his boss's head and plead his case to the CEO.

What did Lawrence do? Instead of blowing up at James, he sat down with his rebellious direct report and talked over not just the decision to close the division but also James's future. He explained to James how moving to another division would help him develop new skills. It would make him a better leader and teach him more about the company's business.

Lawrence acted more like a counselor than a traditional boss. He listened to James's concerns and hopes, and he shared his own. He said he believed James had grown stale in his current job; it was, after all, the only place he'd worked in the company. He predicted that James would blossom in a new role.

The conversation then took a practical turn. James had not yet had his meeting with the CEO—the one he had impetuously demanded when he heard of his division's closing. Knowing this—and also knowing that the CEO unwaveringly supported the closing—Lawrence took the time to coach James on how to present his case in that meeting. "You don't get an audience with the CEO very often," he noted, "let's make sure you impress him with your thoughtfulness." He advised James not to plead his personal case but to focus on the business unit: "If he thinks you're in there for your own glory, he'll throw you out faster than you walked through the door." And he urged him to put his ideas in writing; the CEO always appreciated that.

Lawrence's reason for coaching instead of scolding? "James is a good guy, very talented and promising," the executive explained to us, "and I don't want this to derail his career. I want him to stay with the company, I want him to work out, I want him to learn, I want him to benefit and grow. Just because he screwed up doesn't mean he's terrible."

Lawrence's actions illustrate the coaching style par excellence. Coaching leaders help employees identify their unique strengths and weaknesses and tie them to their personal and career aspirations. They encourage employees to establish long-term development goals and help them conceptualize a plan for attaining them. They make agreements with their employees about their role and responsibilities in enacting development plans, and they give plentiful instruction and feedback. Coaching leaders excel at delegating; they give employees challenging assignments, even if that means the tasks won't be accomplished quickly. In other words, these leaders are willing to put up with short-term failure if it furthers long-term learning.

Of the six styles, our research found that the coaching style is used least often. Many leaders told us they don't have the time in this high-pressure economy for the slow and tedious work of teaching people and helping them grow. But after a first session, it takes little or no extra time. Leaders who ignore this style are passing up a powerful tool: its impact on climate and performance are markedly positive.

Admittedly, there is a paradox in coaching's positive effect on business performance because coaching focuses primarily on personal development, not on immediate work-related tasks. Even so, coaching improves results. The reason: it requires constant dialogue, and that dialogue has a way of pushing up every driver of climate. Take flexibility. When an employee knows his boss watches him and cares about what he does, he feels free to experiment. After all, he's sure to get quick and constructive feedback. Similarly, the ongoing dialogue of coaching guarantees that people know what is expected of them and how their work fits into a larger vision or strategy. That affects responsibility and clarity. As for commitment, coaching helps there, too, because the style's implicit message is, "I believe in you, I'm investing in you, and I expect your best efforts." Employees very often rise to that challenge with their heart, mind, and soul.

The coaching style works well in many business situations, but it is perhaps most effective when people on the receiving end are "up for it." For instance, the coaching style works particularly well when employees are already aware of their weaknesses and would like to improve their performance. Similarly, the style works well when employees realize how cultivating new abilities can help them advance. In short, it works best with employees who want to be coached.

By contrast, the coaching style makes little sense when employees, for whatever reason, are resistant to learning or changing their ways. And it flops if the leader lacks the expertise to help the employee along. The fact is, many managers are unfamiliar with or simply inept at coaching, particularly when it comes to giving ongoing performance feedback that motivates rather than creates fear or apathy. Some companies have realized the positive impact of the style and are trying to make it a core competence. At some companies, a significant portion of annual bonuses are tied to an executive's development of his or her direct reports. But many organizations have yet to take full advantage of this leadership style. Although the coaching style may not scream "bottom-line results," it delivers them.

Leaders Need Many Styles

Many studies, including this one, have shown that the more styles a leader exhibits, the better. Leaders who have mastered four or more—especially the authoritative, democratic, affiliative, and coaching styles—have the very best climate and business performance. And the most effective leaders switch flexibly among the leadership styles as needed. Although that may sound daunting, we witnessed it more often than you might guess, at both large corporations and tiny startups, by seasoned veterans who could explain exactly how and why they lead and by entrepreneurs who claim to lead by gut alone.

Such leaders don't mechanically match their style to fit a checklist of situations—they are far more fluid. They are exquisitely sensitive to the impact they are having on others and seamlessly adjust their style to get the best results. These are leaders, for example, who can read in the first minutes of conversation that a talented but underperforming employee has been demoralized by an unsympathetic, do-it-the-way-I-tell-you manager and needs to be inspired through a reminder of why her work matters. Or that leader might choose to reenergize the employee by asking her about her dreams and aspirations and finding ways to make her job more challenging. Or that initial conversation might signal that the employee needs an ultimatum: improve or leave.

For an example of fluid leadership in action, consider Joan, the general manager of a major division at a global food and beverage company. Joan was appointed to her job while the division was in a deep crisis. It had not made its profit targets for six years; in the most recent year, it had missed by $50 million. Morale among the top management team was miserable; mistrust and resentments were rampant. Joan's directive from above was clear: turn the division around.

Joan did so with a nimbleness in switching among leadership styles that is rare. From the start, she realized she had a short window to demonstrate effective leadership and to establish rapport and trust. She also knew that she urgently needed to be informed about what was not working, so her first task was to listen to key people.

Her first week on the job she had lunch and dinner meetings with each member of the management team. Joan sought to get each person's understanding of the current situation. But her focus was not so much on learning how each person diagnosed the problem as on getting to know each manager as a person. Here Joan employed the affiliative style: She explored their lives, dreams, and aspirations.

She also stepped into the coaching role, looking for ways she could help the team members achieve what they wanted in their careers. For instance, one manager who had been getting feedback that he was a poor team player confided his worries to her. He thought he was a good team member, but he was plagued by persistent complaints. Recognizing that he was a talented executive and a valuable asset to the company, Joan made an agreement with him to point out (in private) when his actions undermined his goal of being seen as a team player.

She followed the one-on-one conversations with a three-day off-site meeting. Her goal here was team building, so that everyone would own whatever solution for the business problems emerged. Her initial stance at the off-site meeting was that of a democratic leader. She encouraged everyone to express freely their frustrations and complaints.

The next day, Joan had the group focus on solutions: each person made three specific proposals about what needed to be done. As Joan clustered the suggestions, a natural consensus emerged about priorities for the business, such as cutting costs. As the group came up with specific action plans, Joan got the commitment and buy-in she sought.

With that vision in place, Joan shifted into the authoritative style, assigning accountability for each follow-up step to specific executives and holding them responsible for their accomplishment. For example, the division had been dropping prices on products without increasing its volume. One obvious solution was to raise prices, but the previous VP of sales had dithered and had let the problem fester. The new VP of sales now had responsibility to adjust the price points to fix the problem.

Over the following months, Joan's main stance was authoritative. She continually articulated the group's new vision in a way that reminded each member of how his or her role was crucial to achieving these goals. And, especially during the first few weeks of the plan's implementation, Joan felt that the urgency of the business crisis justified an occasional shift into the coercive style should someone fail to meet his or her responsibility. As she put it, "I had to be brutal about this follow-up and make sure this stuff happened. It was going to take discipline and focus."

The results? Every aspect of climate improved. People were innovating. They were talking about the division's vision and crowing about their commitment to new, clear goals. The ultimate proof of Joan's fluid leadership style is written in black ink: after only seven months, her division exceeded its yearly profit target by $5 million.

Expanding Your Repertory

Few leaders, of course, have all six styles in their repertory, and even fewer know when and how to use them. In fact, as we have brought the findings of our research into many organizations, the most common responses have been, "But I have only two of those!" and, "I can't use all those styles. It wouldn't be natural."

Such feelings are understandable, and in some cases, the antidote is relatively simple. The leader can build a team with members who employ styles she lacks. Take the case of a VP for manufacturing. She successfully ran a global factory system largely by using the affiliative style. She was on the road constantly, meeting with plant managers, attending to their pressing concerns, and letting them know how much she cared about them personally. She left the division's strategy—extreme efficiency—to a trusted lieutenant with a keen understanding of technology, and she delegated its performance standards to a colleague who was adept at the authoritative approach. She also had a pacesetter on her team who always visited the plants with her.

An alternative approach, and one I would recommend more, is for leaders to expand their own style repertoires. To do so, leaders must first understand which emotional intelligence competencies underlie the leadership styles they are lacking. They can then work assiduously to increase their quotient of them.

For instance, an affiliative leader has strengths in three emotional intelligence competencies: in empathy, in building relationships, and in communication. Empathy—sensing how people are feeling in the moment—allows the affiliative leader to respond to employees in a way that is highly congruent with that person's emotions, thus building rapport. The affiliative leader also displays a natural ease in forming new relationships, getting to know someone as a person, and cultivating a bond. Finally, the outstanding affiliative leader has mastered the art of interpersonal communication, particularly in saying just the right thing or making the apt symbolic gesture at just the right moment.

So if you are primarily a pacesetting leader who wants to be able to use the affiliative style more often, you would need to improve your level of empathy and, perhaps, your skills at building

Growing Your Emotional Intelligence

Unlike IQ, which is largely genetic—it changes little from childhood—the skills of emotional intelligence can be learned at any age. It's not easy, however. Growing your emotional intelligence takes practice and commitment. But the payoffs are well worth the investment.

Consider the case of a marketing director for a division of a global food company. Jack, as I'll call him, was a classic pacesetter: high-energy, always striving to find better ways to get things done, and too eager to step in and take over when, say, someone seemed about to miss a deadline. Worse, Jack was prone to pounce on anyone who didn't seem to meet his standards, flying off the handle if a person merely deviated from completing a job in the order Jack thought best.

Jack's leadership style had a predictably disastrous impact on climate and business results. After two years of stagnant performance, Jack's boss suggested he seek out a coach. Jack wasn't pleased but, realizing his own job was on the line, he complied.

The coach, an expert in teaching people how to increase their emotional intelligence, began with a 360-degree evaluation of Jack. A diagnosis from multiple viewpoints is essential in improving emotional intelligence because those who need the most help usually have blind spots. In fact, our research found that top-performing leaders overestimate their strengths on, at most, one emotional intelligence ability, whereas poor performers overrate themselves on four or more. Jack was not that far off, but he did rate himself more glowingly than his direct reports, who gave him especially low grades on emotional self-control and empathy.

Initially, Jack had some trouble accepting the feedback data. But when his coach showed him how those weaknesses were tied to his inability to display leadership styles dependent on those competencies—especially the authoritative, affiliative, and coaching styles—Jack realized he had to improve if he wanted to advance in the company. Making such a connection is essential. The reason: improving emotional intelligence isn't done in a weekend or during a seminar—it takes diligent practice on the job, over several months. If people do not see the value of the change, they will not make that effort.

Once Jack zeroed in on areas for improvement and committed himself to making the effort, he and his coach worked up a plan to turn his day-to-day job into a learning laboratory. For instance, Jack discovered he was empathetic when things were calm, but in a crisis, he tuned out others. This tendency hampered his ability to listen to what people were telling him in the very moments he most needed to do so. Jack's plan required him to focus on his behavior during tough situations. As soon as he felt himself tensing up, his job was to immediately step back, let the other person speak, and then ask clarifying questions. The point was to not act judgmental or hostile under pressure.

The change didn't come easily, but with practice Jack learned to defuse his flare-ups by entering into a dialogue instead of launching a harangue. Although he didn't always agree with them, at least he gave people a chance to make their case. At the same time, Jack also practiced giving his direct reports more positive feedback and reminding them of how their work contributed to the group's mission. And he restrained himself from micromanaging them.

Jack met with his coach every week or two to review his progress and get advice on specific problems. For instance, occasionally Jack would find himself falling back on his old pacesetting tactics—cutting people off, jumping in to take over, and blowing up in a rage. Almost immediately, he would regret it. So he and his coach dissected those relapses to figure out what triggered the old ways and what to do the next time a similar moment arose. Such "relapse prevention" measures inoculate people against future lapses or just giving up. Over a six-month period, Jack made real improvement. His own records showed he had reduced the number of flare-ups from one or more a day at the beginning to just one or two a month. The climate had improved sharply, and the division's numbers were starting to creep upward.

Why does improving an emotional intelligence competence take months rather than days? Because the emotional centers of the brain, not just the neocortex, are involved. The neocortex, the

(*continued*)

> ### Growing Your Emotional Intelligence (*continued*)
>
> thinking brain that learns technical skills and purely cognitive abilities, gains knowledge very quickly, but the emotional brain does not. To master a new behavior, the emotional centers need repetition and practice. Improving your emotional intelligence, then, is akin to changing your habits. Brain circuits that carry leadership habits have to unlearn the old ones and replace them with the new. The more often a behavioral sequence is repeated, the stronger the underlying brain circuits become. At some point, the new neural pathways become the brain's default option. When that happened, Jack was able to go through the paces of leadership effortlessly, using styles that worked for him—and the whole company.

relationships or communicating effectively. As another example, an authoritative leader who wants to add the democratic style to his repertory might need to work on the capabilities of collaboration and communication. Such advice about adding capabilities may seem simplistic—"Go change yourself"—but enhancing emotional intelligence is entirely possible with practice. (For more on how to improve emotional intelligence, see the sidebar "Growing Your Emotional Intelligence.")

More Science, Less Art

Like parenthood, leadership will never be an exact science. But neither should it be a complete mystery to those who practice it. In recent years, research has helped parents understand the genetic, psychological, and behavioral components that affect their "job performance." With our new research, leaders, too, can get a clearer picture of what it takes to lead effectively. And perhaps as important, they can see how they can make that happen.

The business environment is continually changing, and a leader must respond in kind. Hour to hour, day to day, week to week, executives must play their leadership styles like a pro—using the right one at just the right time and in the right measure. The payoff is in the results.

Originally published in March–April 2000. Reprint R00204

2

The Power of Small Wins

by Teresa M. Amabile and
Steven J. Kramer

What is the best way to drive innovative work inside organizations? Important clues hide in the stories of world-renowned creators. It turns out that ordinary scientists, marketers, programmers, and other unsung knowledge workers, whose jobs require creative productivity every day, have more in common with famous innovators than most managers realize. The workday events that ignite their emotions, fuel their motivation, and trigger their perceptions are fundamentally the same.

The Double Helix, James Watson's 1968 memoir about discovering the structure of DNA, describes the roller coaster of emotions he and Francis Crick experienced through the progress and setbacks of the work that eventually earned them the Nobel Prize. After the excitement of their first attempt to build a DNA model, Watson and Crick noticed some serious flaws. According to Watson, "Our first minutes with the models . . . were not joyous." Later that evening, "a shape began to emerge which brought back our spirits." But when they showed their "breakthrough" to colleagues, they found that their model would not work. Dark days of doubt and ebbing motivation followed. When the duo finally had their bona fide breakthrough, and their colleagues found no fault with it, Watson wrote, "My morale skyrocketed, for I suspected that we now had the answer to the riddle." Watson and Crick were so driven by this success that they practically lived in the lab, trying to complete the work.

Throughout these episodes, Watson and Crick's progress—or lack thereof—ruled their reactions. In our recent research on creative work inside businesses, we stumbled upon a remarkably similar phenomenon. Through exhaustive analysis of diaries kept by knowledge workers, we discovered the *progress principle*: Of all the things that can boost emotions, motivation, and perceptions during a workday, the single most important is making progress in meaningful work. And the more frequently people experience that sense of progress, the more likely they are to be creatively productive in the long run. Whether they are trying to solve a major scientific mystery or simply produce a high-quality product or service, everyday progress—even a small win—can make all the difference in how they feel and perform.

The power of progress is fundamental to human nature, but few managers understand it or know how to leverage progress to boost motivation. In fact, work motivation has been a subject of long-standing debate. In a survey asking about the keys to motivating workers, we found that some managers ranked recognition for good work as most important, while others put more stock in tangible incentives. Some focused on the value of interpersonal support, while still others thought clear goals were the answer. Interestingly, very few of our surveyed managers ranked progress first. (See the sidebar "A Surprise for Managers.")

Idea in Brief

What could be more important for managers than increasing their teams' productivity? Yet most managers labor under misconceptions about what motivates employees—particularly knowledge workers—to do their best work.

On the basis of more than a decade of research, which included a deep analysis of daily diaries kept by teammates on creative projects, the authors clarify the matter once and for all: What motivates people on a day-to-day basis is the sense that they are making progress.

Managers who take this finding to heart will easily see the corollary: The best thing they can do for their people is provide the catalysts and nourishers that allow projects to move forward while removing the obstacles and toxins that result in setbacks. That is easily said, but for most managers it will require a new perspective and new behaviors. A simple checklist, consulted daily, can help make those habitual.

In this article, we share what we have learned about the power of progress and how managers can leverage it. We spell out how a focus on progress translates into concrete managerial actions and provide a checklist to help make such behaviors habitual. But to clarify why those actions are so potent, we first describe our research and what the knowledge workers' diaries revealed about their *inner work lives*.

Inner Work Life and Performance

For nearly 15 years, we have been studying the psychological experiences and the performance of people doing complex work inside organizations. Early on, we realized that a central driver of creative, productive performance was the quality of a person's inner work life—the mix of emotions, motivations, and perceptions over the course of a workday. How happy workers feel; how motivated they are by an intrinsic interest in the work; how

A Surprise for Managers

In a 1968 issue of HBR, Frederick Herzberg published a now-classic article titled "One More Time: How Do You Motivate Employees?" Our findings are consistent with his message: People are most satisfied with their jobs (and therefore most motivated) when those jobs give them the opportunity to experience achievement.

The diary research we describe in this article—in which we microscopically examined the events of thousands of workdays, in real time—uncovered the mechanism underlying the sense of achievement: making consistent, meaningful progress.

But managers seem not to have taken Herzberg's lesson to heart. To assess contemporary awareness of the importance of daily work progress, we recently administered a survey to 669 managers of varying levels from dozens of companies around the world. We asked about the managerial tools that can affect employees' motivation and emotions. The respondents ranked five tools—support for making progress in the work, recognition for good work, incentives, interpersonal support, and clear goals—in order of importance.

Fully 95% of the managers who took our survey would probably be surprised to learn that supporting progress is the primary way to elevate motivation—because that's the percentage that failed to rank progress number one. In fact, only 35 managers ranked progress as the number one motivator—a mere 5%. The vast majority of respondents ranked support for making progress dead last as a motivator and third as an influence on emotion. They ranked "recognition for good work (either public or private)" as the most important factor in motivating workers and making them happy. In our diary study, recognition certainly did boost inner work life. But it wasn't nearly as prominent as progress. Besides, without work achievements, there is little to recognize.

positively they view their organization, their management, their team, their work, and themselves—all these combine either to push them to higher levels of achievement or to drag them down.

To understand such interior dynamics better, we asked members of project teams to respond individually to an end-of-day email survey during the course of the project—just over four months, on average. (For more on this research, see our article "Inner Work Life: Understanding the Subtext of Business Performance," HBR, May 2007.) The projects—inventing kitchen gadgets, managing product lines of cleaning tools, and solving complex IT problems for a hotel empire, for example—all involved creativity. The daily survey inquired about participants' emotions and moods, motivation levels, and perceptions of the work environment that day, as well as what work they did and what events stood out in their minds.

Twenty-six project teams from seven companies participated, comprising 238 individuals. This yielded nearly 12,000 diary entries. Naturally, every individual in our population experienced ups and downs. Our goal was to discover the states of inner work life and the workday events that correlated with the highest levels of creative output.

In a dramatic rebuttal to the commonplace claim that high pressure and fear spur achievement, we found that, at least in the realm of knowledge work, people are more creative and productive when their inner work lives are positive—when they feel happy, are intrinsically motivated by the work itself, and have positive perceptions of their colleagues and the organization. Moreover, in those positive states, people are more committed to the work and more collegial toward those around them. Inner work life, we saw, can fluctuate from one day to the next—sometimes wildly—and performance along with it. A person's inner work life on a given day fuels his or her performance for the day and can even affect performance the *next* day.

Once this *inner work life effect* became clear, our inquiry turned to whether and how managerial action could set it in motion. What events could evoke positive or negative emotions, motivations, and perceptions? The answers were tucked within our research participants' diary entries. There are predictable triggers that inflate or deflate inner work life, and, even accounting for variation among individuals, they are pretty much the same for everyone.

The Power of Progress

Our hunt for inner work life triggers led us to the progress principle. When we compared our research participants' best and worst days (based on their overall mood, specific emotions, and motivation levels), we found that the most common event triggering a "best day" was any progress in the work by the individual or the team. The most common event triggering a "worst day" was a setback.

Consider, for example, how progress relates to one component of inner work life: overall mood ratings. Steps forward occurred on 76% of people's best-mood days. By contrast, setbacks occurred on only 13% of those days. (See the exhibit "What happens on good days and bad days?")

Two other types of inner work life triggers also occur frequently on best days: *Catalysts*, actions that directly support work, including help from a person or group, and *nourishers*, events such as shows of respect and words of encouragement. Each has an opposite: *Inhibitors*, actions that fail to support or actively hinder work, and *toxins*, discouraging or undermining events. Whereas

What happens on good days and bad days?

Progress—even a small step forward—occurs on many of the days people report being in a good mood. Events on bad days—setbacks and other hindrances—are nearly the mirror image of those on good days.

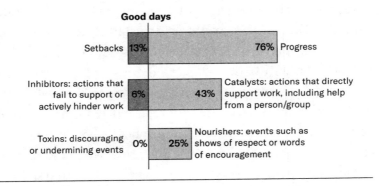

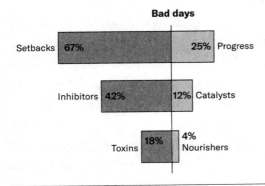

catalysts and inhibitors are directed at the project, nourishers and toxins are directed at the person. Like setbacks, inhibitors and toxins are rare on days of great inner work life.

Events on worst-mood days are nearly the mirror image of those on best-mood days. Here, setbacks predominated, occurring on 67% of those days; progress occurred on only 25%

of them. Inhibitors and toxins also marked many worst-mood days, and catalysts and nourishers were rare.

This is the progress principle made visible: If a person is motivated and happy at the end of the workday, it's a good bet that he or she made some progress. If the person drags out of the office disengaged and joyless, a setback is most likely to blame.

When we analyzed all 12,000 daily surveys filled out by our participants, we discovered that progress and setbacks influence all three aspects of inner work life. On days when they made progress, our participants reported more positive *emotions*. They not only were in a more upbeat mood in general but also expressed more joy, warmth, and pride. When they suffered setbacks, they experienced more frustration, fear, and sadness.

Motivations were also affected: On progress days, people were more intrinsically motivated—by interest in and enjoyment of the work itself. On setback days, they were not only less intrinsically motivated but also less extrinsically motivated by recognition. Apparently, setbacks can lead a person to feel generally apathetic and disinclined to do the work at all.

Perceptions differed in many ways, too. On progress days, people perceived significantly more positive challenge in their work. They saw their teams as more mutually supportive and reported more positive interactions between the teams and their supervisors. On a number of dimensions, perceptions suffered when people encountered setbacks. They found less positive challenge in the work, felt that they had less freedom in carrying it out, and reported that they had insufficient resources. On setback days, participants perceived both their teams and their supervisors as less supportive.

To be sure, our analyses establish correlations but do not prove causality. Were these changes in inner work life the result of progress and setbacks, or was the effect the other way around? The numbers alone cannot answer that. However, we do know, from reading thousands of diary entries, that more-positive perceptions, a sense of accomplishment, satisfaction, happiness, and even elation often followed progress. Here's a typical post-progress entry, from a programmer: "I smashed that bug that's been frustrating me for almost a calendar week. That may not be an event to you, but I live a very drab life, so I'm all hyped."

Likewise, we saw that deteriorating perceptions, frustration, sadness, and even disgust often followed setbacks. As another participant, a product marketer, wrote, "We spent a lot of time updating the Cost Reduction project list, and after tallying all the numbers, we are still coming up short of our goal. It is discouraging to not be able to hit it after all the time spent and hard work."

Almost certainly, the causality goes both ways, and managers can use this feedback loop between progress and inner work life to support both.

Minor Milestones

When we think about progress, we often imagine how good it feels to achieve a long-term goal or experience a major breakthrough. These big wins are great—but they are relatively rare. The good news is that even small wins can boost inner work life tremendously. Many of the progress events our research participants reported represented only minor steps forward. Yet they often evoked outsize positive reactions. Consider this diary entry from a programmer in a high-tech company, which was accompanied by very positive self-ratings of her emotions, motivations, and perceptions that day: "I figured out why something was not working correctly. I felt relieved and happy because this was a minor milestone for me."

Even ordinary, incremental progress can increase people's engagement in the work and their happiness during the workday. Across all types of events our participants reported, a notable proportion (28%) of incidents that had a minor impact on the project had a major impact on people's feelings about it. Because inner work life has such a potent effect on creativity and productivity, and because small but consistent steps forward, shared by many people, can accumulate into excellent execution, progress events that often go unnoticed are critical to the overall performance of organizations.

Unfortunately, there is a flip side. Small losses or setbacks can have an extremely negative effect on inner work life. In fact, our study and research by others show that negative events can have a more powerful impact than positive ones. Consequently, it is especially important for managers to minimize daily hassles.

Progress in Meaningful Work

We've shown how gratifying it is for workers when they are able to chip away at a goal, but recall what we said earlier: The key to motivating performance is supporting progress in *meaningful* work. Making headway boosts your inner work life, but only if the work matters to you.

Think of the most boring job you've ever had. Many people nominate their first job as a teenager—washing pots and pans in a restaurant kitchen, for example, or checking coats at a museum. In jobs like those, the power of progress seems elusive. No matter how hard you work, there are always more pots to wash and coats to check; only punching the time clock at the end of the day or getting the paycheck at the end of the week yields a sense of accomplishment.

In jobs with much more challenge and room for creativity, like the ones our research participants had, simply "making progress"—getting tasks done—doesn't guarantee a good inner work life, either. You may have experienced this rude fact in your own job, on days (or in projects) when you felt demotivated, devalued, and frustrated, even though you worked hard and got things done. The likely cause is your perception of the completed tasks as peripheral or irrelevant. For the progress principle to operate, the work must be meaningful to the person doing it.

In 1983, Steve Jobs was trying to entice John Sculley to leave a wildly successful career at PepsiCo to become Apple's new CEO. Jobs reportedly asked him, "Do you want to spend the rest of your life selling sugared water or do you want a chance to change the world?" In making his pitch, Jobs leveraged a potent psychological force: the deep-seated human desire to do meaningful work.

Fortunately, to feel meaningful, work doesn't have to involve putting the first personal computers in the hands of ordinary people, or alleviating poverty, or helping to cure cancer. Work with less profound importance to society can matter if it contributes value to something or someone important to the worker. Meaning can be as simple as making a useful and high-quality product for a customer or providing a genuine service for a community. It can be supporting a colleague or boosting an organization's profits by reducing inefficiencies in a production process. Whether the goals are lofty or modest,

How Work Gets Stripped of Its Meaning

Diary entries from 238 knowledge workers who were members of creative project teams revealed four primary ways in which managers unwittingly drain work of its meaning.

1. *Managers may dismiss the importance of employees' work or ideas.* Consider the case of Richard, a senior lab technician at a chemical company, who found meaning in helping his new-product development team solve complex technical problems. However, in team meetings over the course of a three-week period, Richard perceived that his team leader was ignoring his suggestions and those of his teammates. As a result, he felt that his contributions were not meaningful, and his spirits flagged. When at last he believed that he was again making a substantive contribution to the success of the project, his mood improved dramatically:

   I felt much better at today's team meeting. I felt that my opinions and information were important to the project and that we have made some progress.

2. *They may destroy employees' sense of ownership of their work.* Frequent and abrupt reassignments often have this effect. This happened repeatedly to the members of a product development team in a giant consumer products company, as described by team member Bruce:

   As I've been handing over some projects, I do realize that I don't like to give them up. Especially when you have been with them from the start and are nearly to the end. You lose ownership. This happens to us way too often.

3. *Managers may send the message that the work employees are doing will never see the light of day.* They can signal this—unintentionally—by shifting their priorities or changing their minds about how something should be done. We saw the latter in an internet technology company after user-interface developer Burt had spent weeks designing seamless

transitions for non-English-speaking users. Not surprisingly, Burt's mood was seriously marred on the day he reported this incident:

Other options for the international [interfaces] were [given] to the team during a team meeting, which could render the work I am doing useless.

4. **They may neglect to inform employees about unexpected changes in a customer's priorities.** Often, this arises from poor customer management or inadequate communication within the company. For example, Stuart, a data transformation expert at an IT company, reported deep frustration and low motivation on the day he learned that weeks of the team's hard work might have been for naught:

Found out that there is a strong possibility that the project may not be going forward, due to a shift in the client's agenda. Therefore, there is a strong possibility that all the time and effort put into the project was a waste of our time.

as long as they are meaningful to the worker and it is clear how his or her efforts contribute to them, progress toward them can galvanize inner work life.

In principle, managers shouldn't have to go to extraordinary lengths to infuse jobs with meaning. Most jobs in modern organizations are potentially meaningful for the people doing them. However, managers can make sure that employees know just how their work is contributing. And, most important, they can avoid actions that negate its value. (See the sidebar "How Work Gets Stripped of Its Meaning.") All the participants in our research were doing work that should have been meaningful; no one was washing pots or checking coats. Shockingly often, however, we saw potentially important, challenging work losing its power to inspire.

Supporting Progress: Catalysts and Nourishers

What can managers do to ensure that people are motivated, committed, and happy? How can they support workers' daily progress? They can use catalysts and nourishers, the other kinds of frequent "best day" events we discovered.

Catalysts are actions that support work. They include setting clear goals, allowing autonomy, providing sufficient resources and time, helping with the work, openly learning from problems and successes, and allowing a free exchange of ideas. Their opposites, inhibitors, include failing to provide support and actively interfering with the work. Because of their impact on progress, catalysts and inhibitors ultimately affect inner work life. But they also have a more immediate impact: When people realize that they have clear and meaningful goals, sufficient resources, helpful colleagues, and so on, they get an instant boost to their emotions, their motivation to do a great job, and their perceptions of the work and the organization.

Nourishers are acts of interpersonal support, such as respect and recognition, encouragement, emotional comfort, and opportunities for affiliation. Toxins, their opposites, include disrespect, discouragement, disregard for emotions, and interpersonal conflict. For good and for ill, nourishers and toxins affect inner work life directly and immediately.

Catalysts and nourishers—and their opposites—can alter the meaningfulness of work by shifting people's perceptions of their jobs and even themselves. For instance, when a manager makes sure that people have the resources they need, it signals to them that what they are doing is important and valuable. When managers recognize people for the work they do, it signals that they are important to the organization. In this way, catalysts and nourishers can lend greater meaning to the work—and amplify the operation of the progress principle.

The managerial actions that constitute catalysts and nourishers are not particularly mysterious; they may sound like Management 101, if not just common sense and common decency. But our diary study reminded us how often they are ignored or forgotten. Even some of the more attentive managers in the companies we studied did not consistently provide catalysts and nourishers. For example, a supply-chain specialist named Michael was, in many ways and on most days, an excellent subteam manager. But he was occasionally so overwhelmed that he became toxic toward his people. When a supplier failed to complete a "hot" order on time and Michael's team had to resort to air shipping to meet the customer's deadline, he realized that the profit margin on the sale would be blown. In irritation, he lashed out at his subordinates, demeaning the solid work they had done and disregarding their own frustration with the supplier. In his diary, he admitted as much:

> As of Friday, we have spent $28,000 in air freight to send 1,500 $30 spray jet mops to our number two customer. Another 2,800 remain on this order, and there is a good probability that they too will gain wings. I have turned from the kindly Supply Chain Manager into the black-masked executioner. All similarity to civility is gone, our backs are against the wall, flight is not possible, therefore fight is probable.

Even when managers don't have their backs against the wall, developing long-term strategy and launching new initiatives can often seem more important—and perhaps sexier—than making sure that subordinates have what they need to make steady progress and feel supported as human beings. But as we saw repeatedly in our research, even the best strategy will fail if managers ignore the people working in the trenches to execute it.

A Model Manager—and a Tool for Emulating Him

We could explain the many (and largely unsurprising) moves that can catalyze progress and nourish spirits, but it may be more useful to give an example of a manager who consistently used those moves—and then to provide a simple tool that can help any manager do so.

Our model manager is Graham, whom we observed leading a small team of chemical engineers within a multinational European firm we'll call Kruger-Bern. The mission of the team's NewPoly project was clear and meaningful enough: develop a safe, biodegradable polymer to replace petrochemicals in cosmetics and, eventually, in a wide range of consumer products. As in many large firms, however, the project was nested in a confusing and sometimes threatening corporate setting of shifting top-management priorities, conflicting signals, and wavering commitments. Resources were uncomfortably tight, and uncertainty loomed over the project's future—and every team member's career. Even worse, an incident early in the project, in which an important customer reacted angrily to a sample, left the team reeling. Yet Graham was able to sustain team members' inner work lives by repeatedly and visibly removing obstacles, materially supporting progress, and emotionally supporting the team.

Graham's management approach excelled in four ways. First, he established a positive climate, one event at a time, which set behavioral norms for the entire team. When the customer complaint stopped the project in its tracks, for example, he engaged immediately with the team to analyze the problem, without recriminations, and develop a plan for repairing the relationship. In doing so, he modeled how to respond to crises in the work: not by panicking or pointing fingers but by identifying problems and their causes, and developing a coordinated action plan. This is both a practical approach and a great way to give subordinates a sense of forward movement even in the face of the missteps and failures inherent in any complex project.

Second, Graham stayed attuned to his team's everyday activities and progress. In fact, the nonjudgmental climate he had established made this happen naturally. Team members updated him frequently—without being asked—on their setbacks, progress, and plans. At one point, one of his hardest-working colleagues, Brady, had to abort a trial of a new material because he couldn't get the parameters right on the equipment. It was bad news, because the NewPoly team had access to the equipment only one day a week, but Brady immediately informed Graham. In his diary entry that evening, Brady noted, "He didn't like the lost week but seemed to understand." That understanding assured Graham's place in the stream of information that would allow him to give his people just what they needed to make progress.

Third, Graham targeted his support according to recent events in the team and the project. Each day, he could anticipate what type of intervention—a catalyst or the removal of an inhibitor; a nourisher or some antidote to a toxin—would have the most impact on team members' inner work lives and progress. And if he could not make that judgment, he asked. Most days it was not hard to figure out, as on the day he received some uplifting news about his bosses' commitment to the project. He knew the team was jittery about a rumored corporate reorganization

The Daily Progress Checklist

Near the end of each workday, use this checklist to review the day and plan your managerial actions for the next day. After a few days, you will be able to identify issues by scanning the boldface words. First, focus on progress and setbacks and think about specific events (catalysts, nourishers, inhibitors, and toxins) that contributed to them. Next, consider any clear inner-work-life clues and what further information they provide about progress and other events. Finally, prioritize for action. The action plan for the next day is the most important part of your daily review: What is the one thing you can do to best facilitate progress?

Progress

Which 1 or 2 events today indicated either a small win or a possible breakthrough? (Describe briefly.)

_____

_____

_____

Setbacks

Which 1 or 2 events today indicated either a small setback or a possible crisis? (Describe briefly.)

_____

_____

_____

Catalysts

- ☐ Did the team have clear short- and long-term **goals** for meaningful work?

- ☐ Did team members have sufficient **autonomy** to solve problems and take ownership of the project?

- ☐ Did they have all of the **resources** they needed to move forward efficiently?

- ☐ Did they have sufficient **time** to focus on meaningful work?

- ☐ Did I give or get them **help** when they needed or requested it? Did I encourage team members to help one another?

- ☐ Did I discuss **lessons** from today's successes and problems with my team?

- ☐ Did I help **ideas** flow freely within the group?

Inhibitors

- ☐ Was there any confusion regarding long- or short-term **goals** for meaningful work?

- ☐ Were team members overly **constrained** in their ability to solve problems and feel ownership of the project?

- ☐ Did they lack any of the **resources** they needed to move forward effectively?

- ☐ Did they lack sufficient **time** to focus on meaningful work?

- ☐ Did I or others fail to provide **help** needed or requested?

- ☐ Did I "punish" failure or neglect to find **lessons** and/or opportunities in problems and successes?

- ☐ Did I or others cut off the presentation or debate of **ideas** prematurely?

(continued)

The Daily Progress Checklist *(continued)*

Nourishers

☐ Did I show **respect** to team members by recognizing their contributions to progress, attending to their ideas, and treating them as trusted professionals?

☐ Did I **encourage** team members who faced difficult challenges?

☐ Did I **support** team members who had a personal or professional problem?

☐ Is there a sense of personal and professional **affiliation** and camaraderie within the team?

Toxins

☐ Did I **disrespect** any team members by failing to recognize their contributions to progress, not attending to their ideas, or not treating them as trusted professionals?

☐ Did I **discourage** a member of the team in any way?

☐ Did I **neglect** a team member who had a personal or professional problem?

☐ Is there tension or **antagonism** among members of the team or between team members and me?

Inner work life

Did I see any indications of the quality of my subordinates' inner work lives today? _____

Perceptions of the work, team, management, firm _____

Emotions _____

Motivation _____

What specific events might have affected inner work life today? _____

Action plan

What can I do tomorrow to strengthen the catalysts and nourishers identified and provide the ones that are lacking? _____

What can I do tomorrow to start eliminating the inhibitors and toxins identified? _____

_____

_____

and could use the encouragement. Even though the clarification came during a well-earned vacation day, he immediately got on the phone to relay the good news to the team.

Finally, Graham established himself as a resource for team members, rather than a micromanager; he was sure to *check in* while never seeming to *check up* on them. Superficially, checking in and checking up seem quite similar, but micromanagers make four kinds of mistakes. First, they fail to allow autonomy in carrying out the work. Unlike Graham, who gave the NewPoly team a clear strategic goal but respected members' ideas about how to meet it, micromanagers dictate every move. Second, they frequently ask subordinates about their work without providing any real help. By contrast, when one of Graham's team members reported problems, Graham helped analyze them—remaining open to alternative interpretations—and often ended up helping to get things back on track. Third, micromanagers are quick to affix personal blame when problems arise, leading subordinates to hide problems rather than honestly discuss how to surmount them, as Graham did with Brady. And fourth, micromanagers tend to hoard information to use as a secret weapon. Few realize how damaging this is to inner work life. When subordinates perceive that a manager is withholding potentially useful information, they feel infantilized, their motivation wanes, and their work is handicapped. Graham was quick to communicate upper management's views of the project, customers' opinions and needs, and possible sources of assistance or resistance within and outside the organization.

In all those ways, Graham sustained his team's positive emotions, intrinsic motivation, and favorable perceptions. His actions serve as a powerful example of how managers at any level can approach each day determined to foster progress.

We know that many managers, however well-intentioned, will find it hard to establish the habits that seemed to come so naturally to Graham. Awareness, of course, is the first step. However, turning an awareness of the importance of inner work life into routine action takes discipline. With that in mind, we developed a checklist for managers to consult on a daily basis (see the exhibit "The Daily Progress Checklist"). The aim of the checklist is managing for meaningful progress, one day at a time.

The Progress Loop

Inner work life drives performance; in turn, good performance, which depends on consistent progress, enhances inner work life. We call this the *progress loop*; it reveals the potential for self-reinforcing benefits.

So, the most important implication of the progress principle is this: By supporting people and their daily progress in meaningful work, managers improve not only the inner work lives of their employees but also the organization's long-term performance, which enhances inner work life even more. Of course, there is a dark side—the possibility of negative feedback loops. If managers fail to support progress and the people trying to make it, inner work life suffers and so does performance; and degraded performance further undermines inner work life.

A second implication of the progress principle is that managers needn't fret about trying to read the psyches of their workers, or manipulate complicated incentive schemes, to ensure that employees are motivated and happy. As long as they show basic respect and consideration, they can focus on supporting the work itself.

To become an effective manager, you must learn to set this positive feedback loop in motion. That may require a significant shift. Business schools, business books, and managers themselves usually focus on managing organizations or people. But if you focus on managing progress, the management of people—and even of entire organizations—becomes much more feasible. You won't have to figure out how to x-ray the inner work lives of subordinates; if you facilitate their steady progress in meaningful work, make that progress salient to them, and treat them well, they will experience the emotions, motivations, and perceptions necessary for great performance. Their superior work will contribute to organizational success. And here's the beauty of it: They will love their jobs.

Originally published in May 2011. Reprint R1105C

3

The Leader as Coach

by Herminia Ibarra and Anne Scoular

Once upon a time, most people began successful careers by developing expertise in a technical, functional, or professional domain. Doing your job well meant having the right answers. If you could prove yourself that way, you'd rise up the ladder and eventually move into people management—at which point you had to ensure that your subordinates had those same answers.

As a manager, you knew what needed to be done, you taught others how to do it, and you evaluated their performance. Command and control was the name of the game, and your goal was to direct and develop employees who understood how the business worked and were able to reproduce its previous successes.

Not today. Rapid, constant, and disruptive change is now the norm, and what succeeded in the past is no longer a guide to what will succeed in the future. Twenty-first-century managers simply don't (and can't!) have all the right answers. To cope with this new reality, companies are moving away from traditional command-and-control practices and toward something very different: a model in which managers give support and guidance rather than instructions, and employees learn how to adapt to constantly changing environments in ways that unleash fresh energy, innovation, and commitment.

The role of the manager, in short, is becoming that of a coach.

This is a dramatic and fundamental shift, and we've observed it firsthand. Over the past decade, we've seen it in our ongoing research on how organizations are transforming themselves for the digital age; we've discerned it from what our executive students and coaching clients have told us about the leadership skills they want to cultivate in themselves and throughout their firms; and we've noticed that more and more of the companies we work with are investing in training their leaders as coaches. Increasingly, coaching is becoming integral to the fabric of a learning culture—a skill that good managers at all levels need to develop and deploy.

We should note that when we talk about coaching, we mean something broader than just the efforts of consultants who are hired to help executives build their personal and professional skills. That work is important and sometimes vital, but it's temporary and executed by outsiders. The coaching we're talking about—the kind that creates a true learning organization—is ongoing and executed by those inside the organization. It's work that all managers should engage in with all their people all the time, in ways that help define the organization's culture and advance its mission. An effective manager-as-coach asks questions instead of providing answers, supports employees instead of judging them, and facilitates their development instead of dictating what has to be done.

This conception of coaching represents an evolution. Coaching is no longer just a benevolent form of sharing what you know with somebody less experienced or less senior, although that remains

Idea in Brief

The Situation
To cope with disruptive change, companies are reinventing themselves as learning organizations. This requires a new approach to management in which leaders serve as coaches to those they supervise.

The Challenge
In this new approach, managers ask questions instead of providing answers, support employees instead of judging them, and facilitate their development instead of dictating what has to be done. But most managers don't feel they have time for that—and they're not very good at it anyway.

The Solution
Companies need to offer their managers the appropriate tools and support to become better coaches. And if they want to be sustainably healthy learning organizations, they must also develop coaching as an organizational capacity.

---

a valuable aspect. It's also a way of asking questions so as to spark insights in the other person. As Sir John Whitmore, a leading figure in the field, defined it, skilled coaching involves "unlocking people's potential to maximize their own performance." The best practitioners have mastered both parts of the process—imparting knowledge and helping others discover it themselves—and they can artfully do both in different situations.

It's one thing to aspire to that kind of coaching, but it's another to make it happen as an everyday practice throughout the many layers of an organization. At most firms, a big gap still yawns between aspiration and practice—and we've written this article to help readers bridge it. We focus first on how to develop coaching as an individual managerial capacity, and then on how to make it an organizational one.

You're Not as Good as You Think

For leaders who are accustomed to tackling performance problems by telling people what to do, a coaching approach often feels too "soft." What's more, it can make them psychologically uncomfortable, because it deprives them of their most familiar management tool: asserting their authority. So they resist coaching—and left to their own devices, they may not even give it a try. "I'm too busy," they'll say, or "This isn't the best use of my time," or "The people I'm saddled with aren't coachable." In Daniel Goleman's classic study of leadership styles, published in *Harvard Business Review* in 2000, leaders ranked coaching as their least-favorite style, saying they simply didn't have time for the slow and tedious work of teaching people and helping them grow.

Even if many managers are unenthusiastic about coaching, most think they're pretty good at it. But a lot of them are not. In one study, 3,761 executives assessed their own coaching skills, and then their assessments were compared with those of people who worked with them. The results didn't align well. Twenty-four percent of the executives significantly overestimated their abilities, rating themselves as above average while their colleagues ranked them in the bottom third of the group. That's a telling mismatch. "If you think you're a good coach but you actually aren't," the authors of the study wrote, "this data suggests you may be a good deal worse than you imagined."

Coaching well can be hard for even the most competent and well-meaning of managers. One of us (Herminia) teaches a class to executives that makes this clear year after year. The executives are given a case study and asked to play the role of a manager who must decide whether to fire or coach a direct report who is not performing up to par. The employee has made obvious errors of judgment, but the manager has contributed significantly to the problem by having alternately ignored and micromanaged him.

When presented with this scenario, nine out of 10 executives decide they want to help their direct report do better. But when they're asked to role-play a coaching conversation with him, they demonstrate much room for improvement. They know what they're supposed to do: "ask and listen," not "tell and sell." But that doesn't come naturally, because deep down they've already made up their minds about the right way forward, usually before they even begin talking to the employee. So their efforts to coach typically consist of just trying to get agreement on what they've already decided. That's not real coaching—and not surprisingly, it doesn't play out well.

Here's roughly how these conversations unfold. The executives begin with an open-ended question, such as "How do you think things are going?" This invariably elicits an answer very different from what they expected. So they reformulate the question, but this, too, fails to evoke the desired response. With some frustration, they start asking leading questions, such as "Don't you think your personal style would be a better fit in a different role?" This makes the direct report defensive, and he becomes even less likely to give the hoped-for answer. Eventually, feeling that the conversation is going nowhere, the executives switch into "tell" mode to get their conclusion across. At the end of the exercise, no one has learned anything about the situation or themselves.

Sound familiar? This kind of "coaching" is all too common, and it holds companies back in their attempts to become learning organizations. The good news, though, is that with the right tools and support, a sound method, and lots of practice and feedback, almost anybody can become a better coach.

Different Ways of Helping

To get managers thinking about the nature of coaching, and specifically how to do it better in the context of a learning organization, we like to present them with the 2 × 2 matrix below. It's a simple but useful tool. One axis shows the information, advice, or expertise that a coach puts in to the relationship with the person being coached; the other shows the motivational energy that a coach *pulls out* by unlocking that person's own insights and solutions.

At the upper left, in quadrant 1, is *directive coaching*, which takes place primarily through "telling." Mentoring falls into this category. Everybody knows what to expect here: A manager with years of accumulated knowledge willingly shares it with a junior team member, and that person listens carefully, hoping to ab-

Styles of coaching

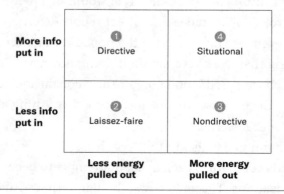

sorb as much knowledge as possible. This approach has a lot to recommend it, but it has some downsides too. Because it consists of stating what to do and how to do it, it unleashes little energy in the person being coached; indeed, it may even depress her energy level and motivation. It also assumes that the boss knows things that the recipient of the coaching does not—not always a safe assumption in a complex and constantly changing work environment. Additionally, because it allows leaders to continue doing what they have always excelled at (solving other people's problems), it does not build organizational capacity well.

That said, coaching is not always the answer. There may be times when all team members are productively getting on with their work, and the right approach to managing them is to leave them alone. This approach, which we call *laissez-faire*, appears in quadrant 2.

At the bottom right, in quadrant 3, is *nondirective coaching*, which is built on listening, questioning, and withholding judgment. Managers here work to draw wisdom, insight, and creativity out of the people they're coaching, with the goal of helping them learn to resolve problems and cope with challenging situations on their own. It's an approach that can be highly energizing for those being coached, but it doesn't come naturally to most managers, who tend to be more comfortable in "tell" mode.

At the top right, in quadrant 4, is *situational coaching*, which represents the sweet spot in our framework. All managers in a learning organization should aspire to become expert at situational coaching—which, as its name suggests, involves striking a fine balance between directive and nondirective styles according to the specific needs of the moment. From our work with experienced executives, we've concluded that managers should first practice nondirective coaching a lot on its own, until it becomes almost second nature, and only then start to balance that newly strengthened ability with periods of helpful directive coaching.

The GROW Model

One of the best ways to get better at nondirective coaching is to try conversing using the GROW model, devised in the 1980s by Sir John Whitmore and others. GROW involves four action steps, the first letters of which give the model its name. It's easy to grasp conceptually, but it's harder to practice than you might imagine, because it requires training yourself to think in new ways about what your role and value are as a leader. The four action steps are these:

Goal. When you begin discussing a topic with someone you're coaching, establish exactly what he wants to accomplish right now. Not what his goals are for the project or his job or his role in the organization, but what he hopes to get out of this particular exchange. People don't do this organically in most conversations, and they often need help with it. A good way to start is to ask something like "What do you want when you walk out the door that you don't have now?"

Reality. With the goal of your conversation established, ask questions rooted in *what, when, where,* and *who,* each of which forces people to come down out of the clouds and focus on specific facts. This makes the conversation real and constructive. You'll notice that we didn't include *why*. That's because asking why demands that people explore reasons and motivations rather than facts. In doing that, it can carry overtones of judgment or trigger attempts at self-justification, both of which can be counterproductive.

During this stage, a good reality-focused question to ask is "What are the key things we need to know?" Attend carefully to how people respond. Are they missing something important? Are they talking about operational issues but forgetting the human side of the equation? Or the reverse? When you ask people to slow down and think in this way, they often lose themselves in contemplation—and then a light comes on, and off they go, engaging with the problem on their own with new energy and a fresh perspective. This step is critical, because it stops people from overlooking pertinent variables and leaping to conclusions. Your job here is just to raise the right questions and then get out of the way.

Options. When people come to you for coaching, they often feel stuck. "There's nothing I can do," they might tell you. Or "I have only one real option." Or "I'm torn between A and B."

At this point your task is to help them think more broadly and more deeply. To broaden the conversation, sometimes it's enough to ask something as simple as "If you had a magic wand, what would you do?" You'd be surprised how freeing many people find that question to be—and how quickly they then start thinking in fresh, productive ways. Once they've broadened their perspective and discovered new options, your job is to prompt them to deepen their thinking, perhaps by encouraging them to explore the upside, the downside, and the risks of each option.

Will. This step also doesn't usually happen organically in conversations, so again most people will need help with it. The step actually has two parts, each involving a different sense of the word *will*.

In the first part you ask, "What will you do?" This encourages the person you're coaching to review the specific action plan that has emerged from your conversation. If the conversation has gone well, she'll have a clear sense of what that plan is. If she doesn't, you'll need to cycle back through the earlier steps of the GROW process and help her define how she'll attack the problem.

The second part involves asking people about their will to act. "On a scale of one to 10," you might ask, "how likely is it that you will do this?" If they respond with an eight or higher, they're probably motivated enough to follow through. If the answer is seven or less, they probably won't. In that case you'll again need to cycle back through the earlier steps of the process, in an effort to arrive at a solution they are more likely to act on.

Of course, workplace coaching usually takes place outside of formal coaching sessions. Most often, it happens in brief exchanges, when a manager might respond to a request for help by posing a single question, such as "What have you already thought of?" or "What really matters here?" When more of those interactions occur—when you notice your managers growing increasingly inquisitive, asking good questions, and working from the premise that they don't have all the answers—you'll know you're on the right track.

Coaching as an Organizational Capacity

So far, we've focused on coaching as a managerial skill. That's a vital first step, but to transform your company into a genuine learning organization, you need to do more than teach individual leaders and managers how to coach better. You also need to make coaching an organizational capacity that fits integrally within your company culture. And to succeed at that, you must effect a cultural transformation that involves the following steps.

Articulate the "why." Managers and professionals are busy people. If coaching strikes them as simply the latest fad being pushed by HR, they will roll their eyes and comply with the requirements as minimally as possible. If you want them to embrace coaching as not just a personal skill but also a source of cultural strength, you'll have to make clear why it's valuable for the business and their own success.

A good "why" inevitably connects coaching to an organization's mission-critical tasks. Consider the example of the international law firm Allen & Overy. When David Morley, then the senior partner, decided to make coaching a key part of the firm's leadership culture, he began talking with his colleagues about the importance of high-value conversations. Morley is an alumnus of one of our (Anne's) leadership coach trainings. "My pitch," he told us, "was this: 'As a senior leader, you have roughly 100 conversations a year that are of particularly high value—in the sense that they will change your life or the life of the person you're talking to. We want to help you acquire the skills to maximize value in those 100 conversations, to unlock previously hidden issues, to uncover new options, and to reveal fresh insights.' That resonated. Almost everybody in a key leadership position at the firm recognized that they struggled with how to make the most of those conversations, and they could readily see that they lacked skills."

Articulating the "why" can also involve helping people see the collateral benefits of coaching. That's what worked at the Berkeley

Coaching 101

Start with a few basic steps.

Assess the situation

Decide what kind of coaching is necessary. Full situational coaching—balancing directive and nondirective coaching moment by moment—isn't always the answer. There will always be scenarios in which people simply need to be told what to do. At other times—if, say, they're struggling with deeply important career decisions—it might be appropriate to offer nondirective coaching but nothing more. It's also possible that your people don't need any coaching right now but would really value an ear later. Ask them.

Listen

Here's a good rule of thumb for most situations: Shut up and listen. Absorb what people tell you, and be alert to what their tone of voice and body language convey. Don't respond as you usually might; instead, listen just to understand. Occasionally repeat back what you hear, to make sure you have it right, but avoid jumping in. Leave room for silence, especially at the end of your conversation. The most important things often emerge from that silence.

Ask open-ended questions

Yes/no questions shut down thinking. Open-ended ones expand it. The coaching thought leader Nancy Kline uses a provocative one that goes roughly like this: "What do you already know, without being aware of it, that you will find out in a year?" But the questions don't have to be complex or clever. Sometimes the simplest—such as "What else?"—are the best. What's vital is that they demonstrate your authentic interest and belief in the person you are coaching. That's something to work hard on, even if the person's performance to date has you doubtful. If you can sincerely suspend judgment, you may be surprised!

> *Practice nondirective coaching*
>
> Practice makes perfect. Try nondirective coaching outside of work—perhaps in some pro bono or other extracurricular role. Practice it in a disciplined, sustained way until you have confidence you're doing it well. You'll know you're getting good when the people you're talking with start to have "Aha!" moments or thank you profusely even though you feel you didn't tell them anything.

Partnership, an international management consultancy, where many partners who have received our training in coaching tell us it has significantly enhanced their ability to serve their clients. According to Mark Fearn, one of the firm's founders, Berkeley partners are now better equipped to respond when clients ask for assistance with big, messy, sometimes ill-defined problems that often extend far beyond the firm's initial brief. Having developed their coaching skills, partners have become better at recognizing situations in which they don't have to provide answers; they understand that in such cases, they may be able to offer more value by listening attentively, asking the right questions, and supporting clients as they work out the best solution. "Now that we've added coaching expertise," Fearn told us, "our task can sometimes be just digging the answer out of them, creating a space to think."

Model the behavior. If you want the people you work with to embrace coaching, you first need to embrace it yourself.

Nobody has done this better than Satya Nadella, the CEO of Microsoft. As noted in a London Business School case study that Herminia cowrote, when Nadella took the reins, in 2014, he was only the third chief executive in the company's four-decade history. During the 14-year tenure of his predecessor, Steve Ballmer, revenue had tripled and profits had doubled, but by the end of that time, the company had lost its momentum. A culture of inspection and judgment prevailed, and the managerial mindset was fixed: Managers evaluated direct reports according to how well they mastered skills and generated numbers that would allow them to reproduce the successes of the past.

This culture had contributed significantly to Microsoft's remarkable run of dominance in the world of personal computing. But as the energy in the tech sector shifted to smartphones and the cloud, the old management practices began to impede progress. By the time Nadella took over, risk aversion and internal politics were hampering cross-divisional collaboration, senior leaders were resisting open-source innovation, and the company's stock price had stalled. Additionally, technologies were changing so quickly that managers often had out-of-date knowledge and practices, but they kept passing these down because that's what they knew how to do.

Nadella quickly realized that Microsoft needed a cultural transformation. To regain its momentum and assert itself as a force in this new landscape, the company had to move away from its entrenched managerial style and instead develop what the Stanford psychologist Carol Dweck has called a growth mindset, in which everybody in the organization was open to constant learning and risk-taking. As Nadella himself aptly put it, the leaders of the company had to shift from being know-it-alls to being "learn-it-alls."

Nadella understood that the process had to start with him, so he began modeling the behaviors he wanted Microsoft's managers to adopt. He solicited thoughts from everybody he talked to and listened empathetically to what they had to say. He asked nondirective questions, demonstrating that his role was to support rather than judge. He encouraged people to be open about their mistakes and to learn from them. "He's with you," said Jean-Phillipe Courtois, a member of his leadership team. "You can feel it. You can see the body language. It doesn't matter if you're a top executive or a first-line seller; he has exactly the same quality of listening."

Modeling is powerful because it shows that a leader walks the talk. Moreover, it builds momentum. Researchers have found that when people are in doubt about what behavior is appropriate, they copy the actions of others—particularly those who have power and status. So it's not surprising that in these times of rapid change, which inevitably bring business uncertainty, employees look to their leaders for cues to follow. If they notice that their leaders are working to foster learning and cultivate the delicate art of leadership as conversation, they will do likewise.

Build capability throughout the organization. After Nadella became Microsoft's CEO, the corporate climate changed and the company's performance surged. But Nadella was not singlehandedly responsible. With more than 130,000 employees, he depended on the members of his leadership team to tailor the growth mindset to the unique requirements of their individual businesses. For Courtois—who in 2016 assumed control of Microsoft's global sales, marketing, and operations—that meant transforming the culture from one of command and control to one of coaching.

Herminia has studied Microsoft's revival in depth, so we have a clear understanding of how things unfolded. Courtois recognized that the "why" of the shift to coaching was Microsoft's move to a cloud-first strategy. The fundamental economics of cloud computing are based on the premise that customers will pay only for the resources they use (how long a server is utilized, say, or how much data bandwidth is being consumed). With revenue growth now depending more heavily on consumption of Microsoft's offerings, everyone at the company had to become adept at having conversations in which they could learn what they did not already know—how to serve the unmet needs of their customers. And with the availability of powerful digital tools that provided everyone with real-time data on key metrics, it no longer made sense for managers to spend their time monitoring and controlling employees. So, after a restructuring effort aimed at giving Microsoft's sales teams the right technical and industry skills to accompany corporate customers as they moved to the cloud, Courtois followed up with workshops, tools, and an online course designed to help the company's managers develop a coaching style of leadership.

"If we want to get the transformation all the way through the organization," he told us, "our biggest challenge is to reboot our people managers. 'People manager' is a job. You're not just a sales manager, where you have a quota, a territory, customers, partners, and goals to achieve. You're actually someone whose mission it is to pick, grow, and motivate the best capabilities to build customer success."

Remove the barriers. As in many organizations, managerial life at Microsoft had a rhythm dictated by quarterly business reviews. One of those, an annual gathering known as the January midyear review, was one of the most visible manifestations of the command-and-control culture.

Over time, the midyear review had developed into a kind of corporate theater in which the C-suite team, adopting an interrogatory stance, would grill senior managers from around the world on their progress and plans. This format of "precision questioning" ended up having "a fear impact on people," said one executive, "because they felt like they were going into that meeting to be judged personally. So they felt they had to paint the best picture they could without showing any mistakes or failures." Stories abounded of senior managers anxiously beginning their preparation well before the December holiday period. In other words, to make a good impression, a raft of the company's most valuable people were diverting more than a month of their time to preparing for an internal review.

As part of the shift to a learning culture, Courtois had already encouraged his team to abandon precision questioning in favor of a more coaching-oriented approach that involved asking questions such as "What are you trying to do?" "What's working?" "What's not working?" and "How can we help?" But old habits die hard. Only after Courtois eliminated the midyear review—thereby removing a significant barrier to change—did everybody understand that he meant business.

Something similar happened at Allen & Overy, where year-end appraisals and rankings had become a largely unproductive ritual. In its push to become a learning organization, the firm recognized that these exercises were a deterrent to the kinds of open and supportive conversations that employees needed both to develop professionally and to advance the organization's mission. It therefore abandoned that performance review system and now trains its partners to engage year-round in coaching conversations with associates, providing them with real-time feedback on their work. Employees report that these conversations create a new and useful level of dialogue about their career development. And once again, there are collateral benefits. Although the program was designed for internal use, it has made the organization's senior leaders more comfortable in conducting unstructured conversations in other contexts, especially during high-stakes client negotiations—and that, in turn, has led to higher revenue and deeper client relationships.

. . .

We live in a world of flux. Successful executives must increasingly supplement their industry and functional expertise with a general capacity for learning—and they must develop that capacity in the people they supervise. No longer can managers simply command and control. Nor will they succeed by rewarding team members mainly for executing flawlessly on things they already know how to do. Instead, with full institutional support, they need to reinvent themselves as coaches whose job it is to draw energy, creativity, and learning out of the people with whom they work.

Originally published in November–December 2019. Reprint R1906G

QUICK READ

Superbosses Aren't Afraid to Delegate Their Biggest Decisions

by Sydney Finkelstein

The answer to excessive micromanaging, we're often told, is to learn to trust our employees, empowering them to make decisions for themselves. Yet that sounds far easier than it actually is. In practice, many bosses fail to delegate because they haven't cultivated a set of underlying mindsets and practices.

Over the past decade, I've studied the world's greatest bosses, extraordinarily successful leaders who have also unleashed vast pipelines of talent. These "superbosses," as I call them, spanned dozens of industries and included legendary figures such as fast-casual restaurant magnate Norman Brinker, packaged foods titan Michael Miles, tech mogul Larry Ellison, hedge fund pioneer Julian Robertson, media icon Oprah Winfrey, and a host of others.

Analyzing these leaders' careers and business practices, I found that superbosses were expert delegators, ceding degrees of authority and control that would send chills down the spines of ordinary bosses. Would you hand a 20-something $25 million in seed capital and tell him to go off on his own to manage it? Julian Robertson did. Would you task a young protégé with generating the main strategy for a new real estate development—only two days before a big presentation with investors? If you're real estate legend Bill Sanders, the answer is yes.

I wondered how superbosses could place such trust in protégés. After reviewing thousands of pages of published sources and interviewing over 200 people, I concluded that innate and unshakable self-confidence certainly played a major role. Yet I discovered an even more important factor. Superbosses embrace a number of specific behaviors and beliefs that enable them to trust their subordinates more deeply, and delegate decision-making authority more aggressively.

Superbosses live to learn and invent. They're die-hard opponents of the status quo. As superboss Lorne Michaels told me: "The show must change. I know it's supposed to be 'must go on,' but 'must change' is important also." Superbosses are constantly pushing themselves to innovate, and they expect employees to work independently and take bold creative risks. As a protégé of advertising legend and superboss Jay Chiat remembered, "Doers were rewarded and anything was possible. If you came to Jay with an idea for how things could be done better, he would say, 'Go ahead and do it.'"

But what if protégés failed in their experiments? The leaders I studied weren't overly concerned. Kyle Craig, who worked with Norman Brinker at Burger King in the 1980s, remembered the superboss openly acknowledging his own failure with an earlier venture, Brink's coffee shop. "He was never unwilling to admit his failures and mistakes, which put people around him very

Idea in Brief

The Problem
Many managers fail to delegate—important decisions, especially—because they don't trust the members of their team to execute.

Why It Matters
No one wins when you micromanage. If you want to challenge the status quo and create lasting value for the business, you need bold ideas and actions from your people.

The Solution
Follow the lead of superbosses like Lorne Michaels of *SNL* and tech mogul Larry Ellison who create the preconditions for trust. Take the risk out of delegation by embracing key behaviors and beliefs including:

- Live to learn and invent (and accept some failure).
- Really know your employees.
- Place clear boundaries around delegation and decision-making.

---

much at ease." If you accept that you will fail from time to time, and that your employees will fail too, it's far easier to relinquish decision-making responsibility—and still sleep at night.

Superbosses really know their employees. They aren't distant bosses, like the hapless leaders on the TV show *Undercover Boss*. Rather, they're what we might call "hands-on delegators." Norman Brinker would show up in restaurants to bus tables with his employees. Newspaper editor and superboss Gene Roberts would invite staffers to his home and stay up until two in the morning talking shop. Deeply committed to coaching and development, these leaders spent a disproportionate amount of time interacting with employees, observing them on the job, and providing valuable feedback.

Regular contact with employees puts superbosses in a perfect position to "trust and verify," as the old motto goes. They can monitor decision-making and enforce accountability on a real-time basis because they're there. "You just knew when you were around Brinker expectations and accountability were givens because of the way he conducted himself," one member of his inner circle recalled.

But superbosses' commitment to highly personal coaching affords another advantage when it comes to delegating. They can also "pre-approve" employees for increasing amounts of responsibility. Superbosses know protégés firsthand. They understand their strengths and weaknesses. They're aware of how much progress their people have made and what responsibility they're ready to shoulder, and they've taken the time to craft customized development plans for them. Delegation thus becomes a far more informed and careful choice than it typically is. In the hands of superbosses, the old motto becomes "Observe, coach, and trust. And then verify."

Superbosses place clear boundaries around delegation and decision-making. Rather than let employees make decisions willy-nilly, these leaders articulate uncompromising visions that they expect employees to internalize and follow. During the execution of work tasks, employees enjoy extraordinary authority over everything except the vision. And superbosses generally stay clear, intervening only to ensure that decisions employees make support their visions and don't conflict with them.

At Lucasfilm, superboss George Lucas trusted his team to define the characters, set designs, and sounds of the original *Star Wars* movie. He didn't micromanage. But he did check in periodically and personally to test employees' inventions against his vision. Because he was so clear about what really mattered—his vision—he could more easily cede control over all else. This is yet another reason why every manager should craft a compelling vision for their teams, no matter where they are in the corporate hierarchy.

If you struggle to devolve decision-making to your team, don't just commit to trusting your employees more. Follow superbosses in creating the preconditions for trust. Embrace a general mindset of constant experimentation and change. Stay close to your employees and become a hands-on delegator. And fence in decision-making by forging and communicating a clear vision. If you lay the groundwork, delegating decisions ceases to be nerve-racking. It becomes what it should be: natural, exciting, and value-creating for bosses and employees alike.

Adapted from hbr.org, August 24, 2016. Reprint H0332C

4

The Set-Up-to-Fail Syndrome

by Jean-François Manzoni and
Jean-Louis Barsoux

When an employee fails—or even just performs poorly—managers typically do not blame themselves. The employee doesn't understand the work, a manager might contend. Or the employee isn't driven to succeed, can't set priorities, or won't take direction. Whatever the reason, the problem is assumed to be the employee's fault—and the employee's responsibility.

But is it? Sometimes, of course, the answer is yes. Some employees are not up to their assigned tasks and never will be, for lack of knowledge, skill, or simple desire. But sometimes—and we would venture to say often—an employee's poor performance can be blamed largely on his boss.

Perhaps "blamed" is too strong a word, but it is directionally correct. In fact, our research strongly suggests that bosses—albeit accidentally and usually with the best intentions—are often complicit in an employee's lack of success. (See the sidebar "About the Research.") How? By creating and reinforcing a dynamic that essentially sets up perceived underperformers to fail. If the Pygmalion effect describes the dynamic in which an individual lives up to great expectations, the set-up-to-fail syndrome explains the opposite. It describes a dynamic in which employees perceived to be mediocre or weak performers live down to the low expectations their managers have for them. The result is that they often end up leaving the organization—either of their own volition or not.

The syndrome usually begins surreptitiously. The initial impetus can be performance related, such as when an employee loses a client, undershoots a target, or misses a deadline. Often, however, the trigger is less specific. An employee is transferred into a division with a lukewarm recommendation from a previous boss. Or perhaps the boss and the employee don't really get along on a personal basis—several studies have indeed shown that compatibility between boss and subordinate, based on similarity of attitudes, values, or social characteristics, can have a significant impact on a boss's impressions. In any case, the syndrome is set in motion when the boss begins to worry that the employee's performance is not up to par.

The boss then takes what seems like the obvious action in light of the subordinate's perceived shortcomings: he increases the time and attention he focuses on the employee. He requires the employee to get approval before making decisions, asks to see more paperwork documenting those decisions, or watches the employee at meetings more closely and critiques his comments more intensely.

These actions are intended to boost performance and prevent the subordinate from making errors. Unfortunately, however,

Idea in Brief

That darned employee! His performance keeps deteriorating—*despite* your close monitoring. What's going on?

Brace yourself: *You* may be at fault, by unknowingly triggering the **set-up-to-fail syndrome**. Employees whom you (perhaps falsely) view as weak performers live down to your expectations. Here's how:

1. You start with a positive relationship.
2. Something—a missed deadline, a lost client—makes you question the employee's performance. You begin micromanaging him.
3. Suspecting your reduced confidence, the employee starts doubting *himself*. He stops giving his best, responds mechanically to your controls, and avoids decisions.
4. You view his new behavior as additional proof of mediocrity—and tighten the screws further.

Why not just fire him? Because you're likely to repeat the pattern with others. Better to *reverse* the dynamic instead. Unwinding the set-up-to-fail spiral actually pays big dividends: Your company gets the best from your employee—and from you.

---

subordinates often interpret the heightened supervision as a lack of trust and confidence. In time, because of low expectations, they come to doubt their own thinking and ability, and they lose the motivation to make autonomous decisions or to take any action at all. The boss, they figure, will just question everything they do—or do it himself anyway.

Ironically, the boss sees the subordinate's withdrawal as proof that the subordinate is indeed a poor performer. The subordinate, after all, isn't contributing his ideas or energy to the organization. So what does the boss do? He increases his pressure and supervision again—watching, questioning, and double-checking everything the subordinate does. Eventually, the subordinate gives up on his dreams of making a

The Set-Up-to-Fail Syndrome

No harm intended: A relationship spirals from bad to worse.

1. Before the set-up-to-fail syndrome begins, the boss and the subordinate are typically engaged in a positive, or at least neutral, relationship.

2. The triggering event in the set-up-to-fail syndrome is often minor or surreptitious. The subordinate may miss a deadline, lose a client, or submit a subpar report. In other cases, the syndrome's genesis is the boss, who distances himself from the subordinate for personal or social reasons unrelated to performance.

3. Reacting to the triggering event, the boss increases his supervision of the subordinate, gives more specific instructions, and wrangles longer over courses of action.

4. The subordinate responds by beginning to suspect a lack of confidence and senses he's not part of the boss's in-group anymore.

    He starts to withdraw emotionally from the boss and from work. He may also fight to change the boss's image of him, reaching too high or running too fast to be effective.

5. The boss interprets this problem-hoarding, overreaching, or tentativeness as signs that the subordinate has poor judgment and weak capabilities. If the subordinate does perform well, the boss does not acknowledge it or considers it a lucky "one off."

    He limits the subordinate's discretion, withholds social contact, and shows, with increasing openness, his lack of confidence in and frustration with the subordinate.

6. The subordinate feels boxed in and under-appreciated. He increasingly withdraws from his boss and from work. He may even resort to ignoring instructions, openly disputing the boss, and occasionally lashing out because of feelings of rejection.

> In general, he performs his job mechanically and devotes more energy to self-protection. Moreover, he refers all nonroutine decisions to the boss or avoids contact with him.
>
> 7. The boss feels increasingly frustrated and is now convinced that the subordinate cannot perform without intense oversight. He makes this known by his words and deeds, further undermining the subordinate's confidence and prompting inaction.
>
> 8. When the set-up-to-fail syndrome is in full swing, the boss pressures and controls the sub- ordinate during interactions. Otherwise, he avoids contact and gives the subordinate routine assignments only.
>
> For his part, the subordinate shuts down or leaves, either in dismay, frustration, or anger.

meaningful contribution. Boss and subordinate typically settle into a routine that is not really satisfactory but, aside from periodic clashes, is otherwise bearable for them. In the worst-case scenario, the boss's intense intervention and scrutiny end up paralyzing the employee into inaction and consume so much of the boss's time that the employee quits or is fired. (For an example of the set-up-to-fail syndrome, see the sidebar "The Set-Up-to-Fail Syndrome.")

Perhaps the most daunting aspect of the set-up-to-fail syndrome is that it is self-fulfilling and self-reinforcing—it is the quintessential vicious circle. The process is self-fulfilling because the boss's actions contribute to the very behavior that is expected from weak performers. It is self-reinforcing because the boss's low expectations, in being fulfilled by his subordinates, trigger more of the same behavior on his part, which in turn triggers more of the same behavior on the part of subordinates. And on and on, unintentionally, the relationship spirals downward.

A case in point is the story of Steve, a manufacturing supervisor for a *Fortune* 100 company. When we first met Steve, he came across as highly motivated, energetic, and enterprising. He was on top of his operation, monitoring problems and addressing them quickly. His boss expressed great confidence in him and gave him an excellent performance rating. Because of his high performance, Steve was chosen to lead a new production line considered essential to the plant's future.

In his new job, Steve reported to Jeff, who had just been promoted to a senior management position at the plant. In the first few weeks of the relationship, Jeff periodically asked Steve to write up short analyses of significant quality-control rejections. Although Jeff didn't really explain this to Steve at the time, his request had two major objectives: to generate information that would help both of them learn the new production process, and to help Steve develop the habit of systematically performing root cause analysis of quality-related problems. Also, being new on the job himself, Jeff wanted to show his own boss that he was on top of the operation.

Unaware of Jeff's motives, Steve balked. Why, he wondered, should he submit reports on information he understood and monitored himself? Partly due to lack of time, partly in response to what he considered interference from his boss, Steve invested little energy in the reports. Their tardiness and below-average quality annoyed Jeff, who began to suspect that Steve was not a particularly proactive manager. When he asked for the reports again, he was more forceful. For Steve, this merely confirmed that Jeff did not trust him. He withdrew more and

About the Research

This article is based on two studies designed to understand better the causal relationship between leadership style and subordinate performance—in other words, to explore how bosses and subordinates mutually influence each other's behavior. The first study, which comprised surveys, interviews, and observations, involved 50 boss-subordinate pairs in four manufacturing operations in *Fortune* 100 companies. The second study, involving an informal survey of about 850 senior managers attending INSEAD executive-development programs over the last three years, was done to test and refine the findings generated by the first study. The executives in the second study represented a wide diversity of nationalities, industries, and personal backgrounds.

more from interaction with him, meeting his demands with increased passive resistance. Before long, Jeff became convinced that Steve was not effective enough and couldn't handle his job without help. He started to supervise Steve's every move—to Steve's predictable dismay. One year after excitedly taking on the new production line, Steve was so dispirited he was thinking of quitting.

How can managers break the set-up-to-fail syndrome? Before answering that question, let's take a closer look at the dynamics that set the syndrome in motion and keep it going.

Deconstructing the Syndrome

We said earlier that the set-up-to-fail syndrome usually starts surreptitiously—that is, it is a dynamic that usually creeps up on the boss and the subordinate until suddenly both of them realize that the relationship has gone sour. But underlying the syndrome are several assumptions about weaker performers that bosses appear to accept uniformly. Our research shows, in fact, that executives typically compare weaker performers with stronger performers using the following descriptors:

- less motivated, less energetic, and less likely to go beyond the call of duty
- more passive when it comes to taking charge of problems or projects
- less aggressive about anticipating problems
- less innovative and less likely to suggest ideas
- more parochial in their vision and strategic perspective
- more prone to hoard information and assert their authority, making them poor bosses to their own subordinates

It is not surprising that on the basis of these assumptions, bosses tend to treat weaker and stronger performers very differently. Indeed, numerous studies have shown that up to 90% of all managers treat some subordinates as though they were members of an in-group, while they consign others to membership in an out-group. Members of the in-group are considered the trusted collaborators and therefore receive more autonomy, feedback, and expressions of confidence from their bosses. The boss-subordinate relationship for this group is one of mutual trust and reciprocal influence. Members of the out-group, on the other hand, are regarded more as hired hands and are managed in a more formal, less personal way, with more emphasis on rules, policies, and authority. (For more on how bosses treat weaker and stronger performers differently, see the chart "In with the in crowd, out with the out.")

In with the in crowd, out with the out

Boss's behavior toward perceived stronger performers	Boss's behavior toward perceived weaker performers
Discusses project objectives, with a limited focus on project implementation. Gives subordinate the freedom to choose his own approach to solving problems or reaching goals.	Is directive when discussing tasks and goals. Focuses on what needs get done as well as how it should get done.
Treats unfavorable variances, mistakes, or incorrect judgments as learning opportunities.	Pays close attention to unfavorable variances, mistakes, or incorrect judgments.
Makes himself available, as in "Let me know if I can help." Initiates casual and personal conversations.	Makes himself available to subordinate on a need-to-see basis. Bases conversations primarily on work-related topics.
Is open to subordinate's suggestions and discusses them with interest.	Has little interest in subordinate's comments or suggestions about how and why work is done.
Gives subordinate interesting and challenging stretch assignments. Often allows subordinate to choose his own assignments.	Reluctantly gives subordinate anything but routine assignments. When handing out assignments, gives subordinate little choice. Monitors subordinate heavily.
Solicits opinions from subordinate on organizational strategy, execution, policy, and procedures.	Rarely asks subordinate for input about organizational or work-related matters.
Often defers to subordinate's opinion in disagreements.	Usually imposes own views in disagreements.
Praises subordinate for work well done.	Emphasizes what the subordinate is doing poorly.

Why do managers categorize subordinates into either in-groups or out-groups? For the same reason that we tend to typecast our family, friends, and acquaintances: it makes life easier. Labeling is something we all do, because it allows us to function more efficiently. It saves time by providing rough-and-ready guides for interpreting events and interacting with others. Managers, for instance, use categorical thinking to figure out quickly who should get what tasks. That's the good news.

The downside of categorical thinking is that in organizations it leads to premature closure. Having made up his mind about a subordinate's limited ability and poor motivation, a manager is likely to notice supporting evidence while selectively dismissing contrary evidence. (For example, a manager might interpret a terrific new product idea from an out-group subordinate as a lucky onetime event.) Unfortunately for some subordinates, several studies show that bosses tend to make decisions about in-groups and out-groups even as early as five days into their relationships with employees.

Are bosses aware of this sorting process and of their different approaches to "in" and "out" employees? Definitely. In fact, the bosses we have studied, regardless of nationality, company, or personal background, were usually quite conscious of behaving in a more controlling way with perceived weaker performers. Some of them preferred to label this approach as "supportive and helpful." Many of them also acknowledged that—although they tried not to—they tended to become impatient with weaker performers more easily than with stronger performers. By and large, however, managers are aware of the controlling nature of their behavior toward perceived weaker performers. For them, this behavior is not an error in implementation; it is intentional.

What bosses typically do *not* realize is that their tight controls end up hurting subordinates' performance by undermining their motivation in two ways: first, by depriving subordinates of autonomy on the job and, second, by making them feel undervalued. Tight controls are an indication that the boss assumes the subordinate can't perform well without strict guidelines. When the subordinate senses these low expectations, it can undermine his self-confidence. This is particularly problematic because numerous studies confirm that people perform up or down to the levels their bosses expect from them or, indeed, to the levels they expect from themselves.[1]

Of course, executives often tell us, "Oh, but I'm very careful about this issue of expectations. I exert more control over my underperformers, but I make sure that it does not come across as a lack of trust or confidence in their ability." We believe what these executives tell us. That is, we believe that they do try hard to disguise their intentions. When we talk to their subordinates, however, we find that these efforts are for the most part futile. In fact, our research shows that most employees can—and do—"read their boss's mind." In particular, they know full well whether they fit into their boss's in-group or out-group. All they have to do is compare how they are treated with how their more highly regarded colleagues are treated.

Just as the boss's assumptions about weaker performers and the right way to manage them explains his complicity in the set-up-to-fail syndrome, the subordinate's assumptions about what the boss is thinking explain his own complicity. The reason? When people perceive disapproval, criticism, or simply a lack of confidence and appreciation, they tend to shut down—a behavioral phenomenon that manifests itself in several ways.

Primarily, shutting down means disconnecting intellectually and emotionally. Subordinates simply stop giving their best. They grow tired of being overruled, and they lose the will to fight for their ideas. As one subordinate put it, "My boss tells me how to execute every detail. Rather than arguing with him, I've ended up wanting to say, 'Come on, just tell me what you want me to do, and I'll go do it.' You become a robot." Another perceived weak performer explained, "When my boss tells me to do something, I just do it mechanically."

Shutting down also involves disengaging personally—essentially reducing contact with the boss. Partly, this disengagement is motivated by the nature of previous exchanges that have tended to be negative in tone. As one subordinate admitted, "I used to initiate much more contact with my boss until the only thing I received was negative feedback; then I started shying away."

Besides the risk of a negative reaction, perceived weaker performers are concerned with not tainting their images further. Following the often-heard aphorism "Better to keep quiet and look like a fool than to open your mouth and prove it," they avoid asking for help for fear of further exposing their limitations. They also tend to volunteer less information—a simple "heads up" from a perceived under-performer can cause the boss to overreact and jump into action when none is required. As one perceived weak performer recalled, "I just wanted to let my boss know about a small matter, only slightly out of the routine, but as soon as I mentioned it, he was all over my case. I should have kept my mouth closed. I do now."

Finally, shutting down can mean becoming defensive. Many perceived underperformers start devoting more energy to self-justification. Anticipating that they will be personally blamed for failures, they seek to find excuses early. They end up spending a lot of time looking in the rearview mirror and less time looking at the road ahead. In some cases—as in the case of Steve, the manufacturing supervisor described earlier—this defensiveness can lead to noncompliance or even systematic opposition to the boss's views. While this idea of a weak subordinate going head to head with his boss may seem irrational, it may reflect what Albert Camus once observed: "When deprived of choice, the only freedom left is the freedom to say no."

The Syndrome Is Costly

There are two obvious costs of the set-up-to-fail syndrome: the emotional cost paid by the subordinate and the organizational cost associated with the company's failure to get the best out of an employee. Yet there are other costs to consider, some of them indirect and long term.

The boss pays for the syndrome in several ways. First, uneasy relationships with perceived low performers often sap the boss's emotional and physical energy. It can be quite a strain to keep up a facade of courtesy and pretend everything is fine when both parties know it is not. In addition, the energy devoted to trying to fix these relationships or improve the subordinate's performance through increased supervision prevents the boss from attending to other activities—which often frustrates or even angers the boss.

Furthermore, the syndrome can take its toll on the boss's reputation, as other employees in the organization observe his behavior toward weaker performers. If the boss's treatment of a subordinate is deemed unfair or unsupportive, observers will be quick to draw their lessons. One outstanding performer commented on his boss's controlling and hypercritical behavior toward another subordinate: "It made us all feel like we're expendable." As organizations increasingly espouse the virtues of learning and empowerment, managers must cultivate their reputations as coaches, as well as get results.

The set-up-to-fail syndrome also has serious consequences for any team. A lack of faith in perceived weaker performers can tempt bosses to overload those whom they consider superior performers; bosses want to entrust critical assignments to those who can be counted on to deliver reliably and quickly and to those who will go beyond the call of duty because of their strong sense of shared fate. As one boss half-jokingly said, "Rule number one: If you want something done, give it to someone who's busy—there's a reason why that person is busy."

An increased workload may help perceived superior performers learn to manage their time better, especially as they start to delegate to their own subordinates more effectively. In many cases, however, these performers simply absorb the greater load and higher stress which, over time, takes a personal toll and decreases the attention they can devote to other dimensions of their jobs, particularly those yielding longer-term benefits. In the worst-case scenario, overburdening strong performers can lead to burnout.

Team spirit can also suffer from the progressive alienation of one or more perceived low performers. Great teams share a sense of enthusiasm and commitment to a common mission. Even when members of the boss's out-group try to keep their pain to themselves, other team members feel the strain. One manager recalled the discomfort experienced by the whole team as they watched their boss grill one of their peers every week. As he explained, "A team is like a functioning organism. If one member is suffering, the whole team feels that pain."

In addition, alienated subordinates often do not keep their suffering to themselves. In the corridors or over lunch, they seek out sympathetic ears to vent their recriminations and complaints, not only wasting their own time but also pulling their colleagues away from productive work. Instead of focusing on the team's mission, valuable time and energy is diverted to the discussion of internal politics and dynamics.

Finally, the set-up-to-fail syndrome has consequences for the subordinates of the perceived weak performers. Consider the weakest kid in the school yard who gets pummeled by a bully. The abused child often goes home and pummels his smaller, weaker siblings. So it is with the people who are in the boss's out-group. When they have to manage their own employees, they frequently replicate the behavior that their bosses show to them. They fail to recognize good results or, more often, supervise their employees excessively.

Breaking Out Is Hard to Do

The set-up-to-fail syndrome is not irreversible. Subordinates can break out of it, but we have found that to be rare. The subordinate must consistently deliver such superior results that the boss is forced to change the employee from out-group to in-group status—a phenomenon made difficult by the context in which these subordinates operate. It is hard for subordinates to impress their bosses when they must work on unchallenging tasks, with no autonomy and limited resources; it is also hard for them to persist and maintain high standards when they receive little encouragement from their bosses.

Furthermore, even if the subordinate achieves better results, it may take some time for them to register with the boss because of his selective observation and recall. Indeed, research shows that bosses tend to attribute the good things that happen to weaker performers to external factors rather than to their efforts and ability (while the opposite is true for perceived high performers: successes tend to be seen as theirs, and failures tend to be attributed to external uncontrollable factors). The subordinate will therefore need to achieve a string of successes in order to have the boss even contemplate revising the initial categorization. Clearly, it takes a special kind of courage, self-confidence, competence, and persistence on the part of the subordinate to break out of the syndrome.

Instead, what often happens is that members of the out-group set excessively ambitious goals for themselves to impress the boss quickly and powerfully—promising to hit a deadline three weeks early, for instance, or attacking six projects at the same time, or simply attempting to handle a large problem without help. Sadly, such superhuman efforts are usually just that. And in setting goals so high that they are bound to fail, the subordinates also come across as having had very poor judgment in the first place.

The set-up-to-fail syndrome is not restricted to incompetent bosses. We have seen it happen to people perceived within their organizations to be excellent bosses. Their mismanagement of some subordinates need not prevent them from achieving success, particularly when they and the perceived superior performers achieve high levels of individual performance. However, those bosses could be even more successful to the team, the organization, and themselves if they could break the syndrome.

Getting It Right

As a general rule, the first step in solving a problem is recognizing that one exists. This observation is especially relevant to the set-up-to-fail syndrome because of its self-fulfilling and self-reinforcing nature. Interrupting the syndrome requires that a manager understand the dynamic and, particularly, that he accept the possibility that his own behavior may be contributing to a subordinate's underperformance. The next step toward cracking the syndrome, however, is more difficult: It requires a carefully planned and structured intervention that takes the form of one (or several) candid conversations meant to bring to the surface and untangle the unhealthy dynamics that define the boss and the subordinate's relationship. The goal of such an intervention is to bring about a sustainable increase in the subordinate's performance while progressively reducing the boss's involvement.

It would be difficult—and indeed, detrimental—to provide a detailed script of what this kind of conversation should sound like. A boss who rigidly plans for this conversation with a subordinate will not be able to engage in real dialogue with him, because real dialogue requires flexibility. As a guiding framework, however, we offer five components that characterize effective interventions. Although they are not strictly sequential steps, all five components should be part of these interventions.

First, the boss must create the right context for the discussion.

He must, for instance, select a time and place to conduct the meeting so that it presents as little threat as possible to the subordinate. A neutral location may be more conducive to open dialogue than an office where previous and perhaps unpleasant conversations have taken place. The boss must also use affirming language when asking the subordinate to meet with him. The session should not be billed as "feedback," because such terms may suggest baggage from the past. "Feedback" could also be taken to mean that the conversation will be one-directional, a monologue delivered by the boss to the subordinate. Instead, the intervention should be described as a meeting to discuss the performance of the subordinate, the role of the boss, and the relationship between the subordinate and the boss. The boss might even acknowledge that he feels tension in the relationship and wants to use the conversation as a way to decrease it.

Finally, in setting the context, the boss should tell the perceived weaker performer that he would genuinely like the interaction to be an open dialogue. In particular, he should acknowledge that he may be partially responsible for the situation and that his own behavior toward the subordinate is fair game for discussion.

Second, the boss and the subordinate must use the intervention process to come to an agreement on the symptoms of the problem.

Few employees are ineffective in all aspects of their performance. And few—if any—employees desire to do poorly on the job. Therefore, it is critical that the intervention result in a mutual understanding of the specific job responsibilities in which the subordinate is weak. In the case of Steve and Jeff, for instance, an exhaustive sorting of the evidence might have led to an agreement that Steve's underperformance was not universal but instead largely confined to the quality of the reports he submitted (or failed to submit). In another situation, it might be agreed that a purchasing manager was weak when it came to finding off-shore suppliers and to voicing his ideas in meetings. Or a new investment professional and his boss might come to agree that his performance was subpar when it came to timing the sales and purchase of stocks, but they might also agree that his financial analysis of stocks was quite strong. The idea here is that before working to improve performance or reduce tension in a relationship, an agreement must be reached about what areas of performance contribute to the contentiousness.

We used the word "evidence" above in discussing the case of Steve and Jeff. That is because a boss needs to back up his performance assessments with facts and data—that is, if the intervention is to be useful. They cannot be based on feelings—as in Jeff telling Steve, "I just have the feeling you're not putting enough energy into the reports." Instead, Jeff needs to describe what a good report should look like and the ways in which Steve's reports fall short. Likewise, the subordinate must be allowed—indeed, encouraged—to defend his performance, compare it with colleagues' work, and point out areas in which he is strong. After all, just because it is the boss's opinion does not make it a fact.

Third, the boss and the subordinate should arrive at a common understanding of what might be causing the weak performance in certain areas.

Once the areas of weak performance have been identified, it is time to unearth the reasons for those weaknesses. Does the subordinate have limited skills in organizing work, managing his time, or working with others? Is he lacking knowledge or capabilities? Do the boss and the subordinate agree on their priorities? Maybe the subordinate has been paying less attention to a particular dimension of his work because he does not realize its importance to the boss. Does the subordinate become less effective under pressure? Does he have lower standards for performance than the boss does?

It is also critical in the intervention that the boss bring up the subject of his own behavior toward the subordinate and how this affects the subordinate's performance. The boss might even try to describe the dynamics of the set-up-to-fail syndrome. "Does my behavior toward you make things worse for you?" he might ask, or, "What am I doing that is leading you to feel that I am putting too much pressure on you?"

This component of the discussion also needs to make explicit the assumptions that the boss and the subordinate have thus far been making about each other's intentions. Many misunderstandings start with untested assumptions. For example, Jeff might have said, "When you did not supply me with the reports I asked for, I came to the conclusion that you were not very proactive." That would have allowed Steve to bring his buried assumptions into the open. "No," he might have answered, "I just reacted negatively because you asked for the reports in writing, which I took as a sign of excessive control."

Fourth, the boss and the subordinate should arrive at an agreement about their performance objectives and on their desire to have the relationship move forward.

In medicine, a course of treatment follows the diagnosis of an illness. Things are a bit more complex when repairing organizational dysfunction, since modifying behavior and developing complex skills can be more difficult than taking a few pills. Still, the principle that applies to medicine also applies to business: Boss and subordinate must use the intervention to plot a course of treatment regarding the root problems they have jointly identified.

The contract between boss and subordinate should identify the ways they can improve on their skills, knowledge, experience, or personal relationship. It should also include an explicit discussion of how much and what type of future supervision the boss will have. No boss, of course, should suddenly abdicate his involvement; it is legitimate for bosses to monitor subordinates' work, particularly when a subordinate has shown limited abilities in one or more facets of his job. From the subordinate's point of view, however, such involvement by the boss is more likely to be accepted, and possibly even welcomed, if the goal is to help the subordinate develop and improve over time. Most subordinates can accept temporary involvement that is meant to decrease as their performance improves. The problem is intense monitoring that never seems to go away.

Fifth, the boss and the subordinate should agree to communicate more openly in the future.

The boss could say, "Next time I do something that communicates low expectations, can you let me know immediately?" And the subordinate might say, or be encouraged to say, "Next time I do something that aggravates you or that you do not understand, can you also let me know right away?" Those simple requests can open the door to a more honest relationship almost instantly.

No Easy Answer

Our research suggests that interventions of this type do not take place very often. Face-to-face discussions about a subordinate's performance tend to come high on the list of workplace situations people would rather avoid, because such conversations have the potential to make both parties feel threatened or embarrassed. Subordinates are reluctant to trigger the discussion because they are worried about coming across as thin-skinned or whiny. Bosses tend to avoid initiating these talks because they are concerned about the way the subordinate might react; the discussion could force the boss to make explicit his lack of confidence in the subordinate, in turn putting the subordinate on the defensive and making the situation worse.[2]

As a result, bosses who observe the dynamics of the set-up-to-fail syndrome being played out may be tempted to avoid an explicit discussion. Instead, they will proceed tacitly by trying to encourage their perceived weak performers. That approach has the short-term benefit of bypassing the discomfort of an open discussion, but it has three major disadvantages.

First, a one-sided approach on the part of the boss is less likely to lead to lasting improvement because it focuses on only one symptom of the problem—the boss's behavior. It does not address the subordinate's role in the underperformance.

Second, even if the boss's encouragement were successful in improving the employee's performance, a unilateral approach would limit what both he and the subordinate could otherwise learn from a more up-front handling of the problem. The subordinate, in particular, would not have the benefit of observing and learning from how his boss handled the difficulties in their relationship—problems the subordinate may come across someday with the people he manages.

Finally, bosses trying to modify their behavior in a unilateral way often end up going overboard; they suddenly give the subordinate more autonomy and responsibility than he can handle productively. Predictably, the subordinate fails to deliver to the boss's satisfaction, which leaves the boss even more frustrated and convinced that the subordinate cannot function without intense supervision.

We are not saying that intervention is always the best course of action. Sometimes, intervention is not possible or desirable. There may be, for instance, overwhelming evidence that the subordinate is not capable of doing his job. He was a hiring or promotion mistake, which is best handled by removing him from the position. In other cases, the relationship between the boss and the subordinate is too far gone—too much damage has occurred to repair it. And finally, sometimes bosses are too busy and under too much pressure to invest the kind of resources that intervention involves.

Yet often the biggest obstacle to effective intervention is the boss's mindset. When a boss believes that a subordinate is a weak performer and, on top of everything else, that person also aggravates him, he is not going to be able to cover up his feelings with words; his underlying convictions will come out in the meeting. That is why preparation for the intervention is crucial. Before even deciding to have a meeting, the boss must separate emotion from reality. Was the situation always as bad as it is now? Is the subordinate really as bad as I think he is? What is the hard evidence I have for that belief? Could there be other factors, aside from performance, that have led me to label this subordinate a weak performer? Aren't there a few things that he does well? He must have displayed above-average qualifications when we decided to hire him. Did these qualifications evaporate all of a sudden?

The boss might even want to mentally play out part of the conversation beforehand. If I say this to the subordinate, what might he answer? Yes, sure, he would say that it was not his fault and that the customer was unreasonable. Those excuses—are they really without merit? Could he have a point? Could it be that, under other circumstances, I might have looked more favorably upon them? And if I still believe I'm right, how can I help the subordinate see things more clearly?

The boss must also mentally prepare himself to be open to the subordinate's views, even if the subordinate challenges him about any evidence regarding his poor performance. It will be easier for the boss to be open if, when preparing for the meeting, he has already challenged his own preconceptions.

Even when well prepared, bosses typically experience some degree of discomfort during intervention meetings. That is not all bad. The subordinate will probably be somewhat uncomfortable as well, and it is reassuring for him to see that his boss is a human being, too.

Calculating Costs and Benefits

As we've said, an intervention is not always advisable. But when it is, it results in a range of outcomes that are uniformly better than the alternative—that is, continued underperformance and tension. After all, bosses who systematically choose either to ignore their subordinates' underperformance or to opt for the more expedient solution of simply removing perceived weak performers are condemned to keep repeating the same mistakes. Finding and training replacements for perceived weak performers is a costly and recurrent expense. So is monitoring and controlling the deteriorating performance of a disenchanted subordinate. Getting results *in spite of* one's staff is not a sustainable solution. In other words, it makes sense to think of the intervention as an investment, not an expense—with the payback likely to be high.

How high that payback will be and what form it will take obviously depend on the outcome of the intervention, which will itself depend not only on the quality of the intervention but also on several key contextual factors: How long has that relationship been spiraling downward? Does the subordinate have the intellectual and emotional resources to make the effort that will be required? Does the boss have enough time and energy to do his part?

We have observed outcomes that can be clustered into three categories. In the best-case scenario, the intervention leads to a mixture of coaching, training, job redesign, and a clearing of the air; as a result, the relationship and the subordinate's performance improve, and the costs associated with the syndrome go away or, at least, decrease measurably.

In the second-best scenario, the subordinate's performance improves only marginally, but because the subordinate received an honest and open hearing from the boss, the relationship between the two becomes more productive. Boss and subordinate develop a better understanding of those job dimensions the subordinate can do well and those he struggles with. This improved understanding leads the boss and the subordinate to explore *together* how they can develop a better fit between the job and the subordinate's strengths and weaknesses. That improved fit can be achieved by significantly modifying the subordinate's existing job or by transferring the subordinate to another job within the company. It may even result in the subordinate's choosing to leave the company.

While that outcome is not as successful as the first one, it is still productive; a more honest relationship eases the strain on both the boss and the subordinate, and in turn on the subordinate's subordinates. If the subordinate moves to a new job within the organization that better suits him, he will likely become a stronger performer. His relocation may also open up a spot in his old job for a better performer. The key point is that, having been treated fairly, the subordinate is much more likely to accept the outcome of the process. Indeed, recent studies show that the perceived fairness of a process has a major impact on employees' reactions to its outcomes. (See "Fair Process: Managing in the Knowledge Economy," by W. Chan Kim and Renée Mauborgne, HBR, July–August 1997.)

Such fairness is a benefit even in the cases where, despite the boss's best efforts, neither the subordinate's performance nor his relationship with his boss improves significantly. Sometimes this happens: The subordinate truly lacks the ability to meet the job requirements, he has no interest in making the effort to improve, and the boss and the subordinate have both professional and personal differences that are irreconcilable. In those cases, however, the intervention still yields indirect benefits because, even if termination follows, other employees within the company are less likely to feel expendable or betrayed when they see that the subordinate received fair treatment.

Prevention Is the Best Medicine

The set-up-to-fail syndrome is not an organizational fait accompli. It can be unwound. The first step is for the boss to become aware of its existence and acknowledge the possibility that he might be part of the problem. The second step requires that the boss initiate a clear, focused intervention. Such an intervention demands an open exchange between the boss and the subordinate based on the evidence of poor performance, its underlying causes, and their joint responsibilities—culminating in a joint decision on how to work toward eliminating the syndrome itself.

Reversing the syndrome requires managers to challenge their own assumptions. It also demands that they have the courage to look within themselves for causes and solutions before placing the burden of responsibility where it does not fully belong. Prevention of the syndrome, however, is clearly the best option.

In our current research, we examine prevention directly. Our results are still preliminary, but it appears that bosses who manage to consistently avoid the set-up-to-fail syndrome have several traits in common. They do not, interestingly, behave the same way with all subordinates. They are more involved with some subordinates than others—they even monitor some subordinates more than others. However, they do so without disempowering and discouraging subordinates.

How? One answer is that those managers begin by being actively involved with all their employees, gradually reducing their involvement based on improved performance. Early guidance is not threatening to subordinates, because it is not triggered by performance shortcomings; it is systematic and meant to help set the conditions for future success. Frequent contact in the beginning of the relationship gives the boss ample opportunity to communicate with subordinates about priorities, performance measures, time allocation, and even expectations of the type and frequency of communication. That kind of clarity goes a long way toward preventing the dynamic of the set-up-to-fail syndrome, which is so often fueled by unstated expectations and a lack of clarity about priorities.

For example, in the case of Steve and Jeff, Jeff could have made explicit very early on that he wanted Steve to set up a system that would analyze the root causes of quality control rejections systematically. He could have explained the benefits of establishing such a system during the initial stages of setting up the new production line, and he might have expressed his intention to be actively involved in the system's design and early operation. His future involvement might then have decreased in such a way that could have been jointly agreed on at that stage.

Another way managers appear to avoid the set-up-to-fail syndrome is by challenging their own assumptions and attitudes about employees on an ongoing basis. They work hard at resisting the temptation to categorize employees in simplistic ways. They also monitor their own reasoning. For example, when feeling frustrated about a subordinate's performance, they ask themselves, "What are the facts?" They examine whether they are expecting things from the employee that have not been articulated, and they try to be objective about how often and to what extent the employee has really failed. In other words, these bosses delve into their own assumptions and behavior before they initiate a full-blown intervention.

Finally, managers avoid the set-up-to-fail syndrome by creating an environment in which employees feel comfortable discussing their performance and their relationships with the boss. Such an environment is a function of several factors: the boss's openness, his comfort level with having his own opinions challenged, even his sense of humor. The net result is that the boss and the subordinate feel free to communicate frequently and to ask one another questions about their respective behaviors before problems mushroom or ossify.

The methods used to head off the set-up-to-fail syndrome do, admittedly, involve a great deal of emotional investment from bosses—just as interventions do. We believe, however, that this higher emotional involvement is the key to getting subordinates to work to their full potential. As with most things in life, you can only expect to get a lot back if you put a lot in. As a senior executive once said to us, "The respect you give is the respect you get." We concur. If you want—indeed, need—the people in your organization to devote their whole hearts and minds to their work, then you must, too.

Originally published in March–April 1998. Reprint 98209

5

The Overcommitted Organization

by Mark Mortensen and
Heidi K. Gardner

A senior executive we'll call Christine is overseeing the launch of Analytix, her company's new cloud-based big-data platform, and she's expected to meet a tight go-live deadline. Until two weeks ago, her team was on track to do that, but it has since fallen seriously behind schedule. Her biggest frustration: Even though nothing has gone wrong with Analytix, her people keep getting pulled into other projects. She hasn't seen her three key engineers for days, because they've been busy fighting fires around a security breach on another team's product. Now she has to explain to the CEO that she can't deliver as promised—at a time when the company badly needs a successful launch.

Christine's story is hardly unique. Across the world, senior managers and team leaders are increasingly frustrated by conflicts arising from what we refer to as multiteaming—having their people assigned to multiple projects simultaneously. But given the significant benefits of multiteaming, it has become a way of organizational life, particularly in knowledge work. It allows groups to share individuals' time and brainpower across functional and departmental lines. It increases efficiency, too. Few organizations can afford to have their employees focus on just one project at a time and sit idle between tasks. So companies have optimized human capital somewhat as they would machines in factories, spreading expensive resources across teams that don't need 100% of those resources 100% of the time. As a result, they avoid costly downtime during projects' slow periods, and they can bring highly specialized experts in-house to dip in and out of critical projects as needed. Multiteaming also provides important pathways for knowledge transfer and the dissemination of best practices throughout organizations.

As clear and quantifiable as these advantages are, the costs are substantial and need to be managed, as Christine would attest. Organizations open themselves up to the risk of transmitting shocks across teams when shared members link the fates of otherwise independent projects. And teams discover that the constant entrance and exit of members weakens group cohesion and identity, making it harder to build trust and resolve issues. Individual employees pay a big price as well. They often experience stress, fatigue, and burnout as they struggle to manage their time and engagement across projects.

Over the past 15 years, we have studied collaboration in hundreds of teams, in settings as varied as professional services, oil and gas, high tech, and consumer goods. By carefully observing people during various stages of project-driven work, we have learned a tremendous amount about multiteaming. In this article we discuss why it is so prevalent in today's economy, examine

Idea in Brief

The Pros
By assigning people to multiple teams at once, organizations make efficient use of time and brainpower. They also do a better job of solving complex problems and sharing knowledge across groups.

The Cons
Competing priorities and other conflicts can make it hard for teams with overlapping membership to stay on track. Group cohesion also suffers. And people who belong to many teams at once may experience burnout, which hurts engagement and performance.

The Fixes
Leaders can mitigate these risks by building trust and familiarity through launches and skills mapping, identifying which groups are most vulnerable to shocks, improving coordination across teams, and carving out more opportunities for learning.

---

the key problems that crop up for organizational and team leaders, and provide recommendations for how to solve them.

Why This Matters Now

Even though assigning employees to multiple projects at once is not new, the practice is especially widespread today. In a survey of more than 500 managers in global companies, we found that 81% of those working on teams worked on more than one concurrently. Other research places the number even higher—for example, 95% in knowledge-intensive industries.

Why is multiteaming practically ubiquitous? For several reasons.

First, organizations must draw on expertise in multiple disciplines to solve many large, complex problems. Businesses are tackling cybersecurity risks that span departments as diverse as finance, supply chain, and travel. Energy companies are coordinating global megaprojects, including the opening of new deep-sea resource fields. Transportation and logistics firms are tasked with getting resources from point A to point B on time, irrespective of how remote those points are or what is being delivered. Large-scale manufacturing and construction endeavors, such as aircraft and city infrastructure projects, require tight collaboration between those producing the work and the agencies regulating it. In such contexts, organizations can't rely on generalists to come up with comprehensive, end-to-end solutions. They must combine the contributions of experts with deep knowledge in various domains. (For more on this, see "Getting Your Stars to Collaborate," HBR, January–February 2017.)

Second, with crowded markets and reduced geographic and industry barriers, organizations now face greater pressure to keep costs down and stretch resources. One client manager in a professional services firm noted, "To be really good stewards of client dollars, we don't want to pay for five weeks of a specialist's time when what we really need is an intense effort from that person in week five." That's why "bench time" between projects and even slow periods during projects have become increasingly rare. The instant people are underutilized, their organizations put them to work on other things. In our research we found that even senior-level managers were flipping among seven or more projects in a single day—and as many as 25 in a given week. Compounding this, technology makes it easier to track downtime—even if it's just minutes—and assign employees work or loop them into projects during any lulls.

Third, organizational models are moving away from hierarchical, centralized staffing to give employees more choice in their projects and improve talent development, engagement, and retention. Indeed, in the gig economy, individuals have greater control than ever over the work they do (think open-source software programmers). This has made leading teams an even more critical skill. (For more on this, see "The Secrets of Great Teamwork," HBR, June 2016.) At the same time, it has brought multiteaming—and the associated risks—to a whole new level. More and more people have at-will contracts and work not only on multiple projects but for multiple organizations. In many cases, companies are sharing team members' time and smarts with market rivals.

Although most managers recognize the increasing prevalence of multiteaming, few have a complete understanding of how it affects their organizations, their teams, and individual employees. For instance, top leaders in one professional services firm were surprised to learn who in their organization was most squeezed by multiteaming. First-year associates worked on as many as six projects in a week, which at a glance seemed like a lot. But the number rose steeply with tenure—employees worked on as many as 15 projects a week once they had reached the six-year mark. More-experienced people were members of fewer concurrent teams, but the more senior they got, the more likely they were to lead many projects at the same time. Interviews revealed that working on multiple teams was stressful—one person likened it to being "slapped about" by different project leaders—despite benefits such as bringing lessons from one project to bear on others.

It's a classic "blind men and elephant problem." Managers see some of the benefits and some of the drawbacks firsthand but rarely all at once, because those things play out through different mechanisms and at different levels. Imagine, for example, a sales

Who takes the hit?

When a couple of teams share many members, a shock to one group severely jolts the other, because people shift their efforts from ongoing work to firefighting.

When many teams share just one or two members, a shock to one group has a minor impact on the others—but the effects ripple throughout the organization.

---

manager who wants to provide better solutions for customers by incorporating insights from her team members' experiences on other projects. That's not going to happen if splitting each individual's time across five projects means her team doesn't have the bandwidth to sit down and share those great ideas in the first place. Or consider a project manager who is thinking about adding a third engineer to his team—just 10% of a full-time equivalent—to reduce the load on his two overworked lead engineers. He may not recognize that this sort of slicing and dicing is the reason his first two engineers are in danger of burnout—they are being pulled into too many competing projects. Examples like these abound.

For the most part, the benefits of multiteaming involve efficiency and knowledge flow, while the costs are largely intra- or interpersonal and psychological. That may be why the costs are tracked and managed less closely, if at all—and why they so often undermine the benefits without leaders' realizing it.

Managing the Challenges

Through our research and consulting, we have identified several ways that both team and organizational leaders can reduce the costs of multiteaming and better capitalize on its benefits. We'll outline them below.

Priorities for team leaders

Coordinating members' efforts (both within and across teams) and promoting engagement and adaptability are the key challenges for team leaders. Focusing on those goals early on, before your team even meets for the first time, will help you establish stronger relationships, reduce coordination costs, ease the friction of transitions, ward off political skirmishes, and identify risks so that you can better mitigate them. Here's how to do it:

Launch the team well to establish trust and familiarity. When fully dedicated to one team, people learn about their teammates' outside lives—family, hobbies, life events, and the like. This enables them to coordinate better (they know, for example, that one teammate is off-line during kids' bedtimes or that another routinely hits the gym during lunch). More important, it forges strong bonds and interpersonal trust, which team members need in order to seek and offer constructive feedback, introduce one another to valuable network connections, and rely on one another's technical expertise.

When multiteaming, in contrast, people tend to be hyperfocused on efficiency and are less inclined to share personal information. If you don't engineer personal interactions *for* them, chances are they'll be left with an anemic picture of their teammates, which can breed suspicion about why others fail to respond promptly, how committed they are to team outcomes, and so on. So make sure team members spend some time in the beginning getting to know their colleagues. This will also help far-flung contributors give one another the benefit of the doubt later on. A Boston-based designer told us about his British counterpart:

> *I used to think that Sylvia was frosty and elitist, because she never jumped into our brainstorming sessions. Instead, she sent missives afterward, sometimes only to the project director. Then we spent a few days working together in person while I was in London, and I came to appreciate that she's an introvert who just needs time to process ideas before responding. Plus, because she had never met any of us, it was really hard for her to keep track of who had said what on the calls; she recognized only the leader's unique accent.*

After the designer shared that "aha" with the team leader, the group switched to video calls so that everyone could see Sylvia's "thinking face" and she could feel confident that she was responding to the right people when making comments.

Formally launching the team—in person, if at all possible—helps a lot, especially if members open up about their own development goals. At McKinsey each team member, including the leader, explains how he or she expects to use that project to build or improve a critical skill. This level of openness not only encourages people to display some vulnerability (which is practically the definition of trust) but also gives members concrete ideas about how they can help one another.

The launch may feel like an unnecessary step if people know one another and everyone is ready to dive in, but research shows that team kickoffs can improve performance by up to 30%, in part because they increase peer-to-peer accountability. By clarifying roles and objectives up front and establishing group norms, you're letting people know what to expect from their colleagues. That's needed on any team, of course, but it's especially critical in organizations where people belong to several teams at once and must absorb *many* sets of roles, objectives, and norms to do good work across the board.

On teams that people frequently join or leave, you'll need to periodically "re-kick" to onboard new members and assess whether agreed-upon processes and expectations still make sense. A good rule of thumb is to do this whenever 15% of the team has changed.

Map everyone's skills. Figure out the full portfolio of capabilities that each person brings to the project—both technical skills and broader kinds of knowledge, such as familiarity with the customer's decision-making process, or a knack for negotiation, or insights about an important target market. Make sure everyone knows how each teammate contributes. This increases the chances that members will learn from one another. The pride people take in sharing their knowledge and the cohesion fostered by peer mentoring are often as valuable as the actual knowledge shared.

As with launching, it's tempting to skip mapping if many members have worked together before. But we've found that even familiar teams are likely to hold outdated assumptions about individuals' potential contributions and often disagree about their teammates' expertise. As a result, they may argue about which roles members should play or bristle at assignments, thinking they're unfair or a bad fit. People may also waste time seeking outside resources when a teammate already has the needed knowledge, which demotivates those whose skills have been overlooked.

Sherif, a tax expert, experienced these problems when he joined with four colleagues to pitch a new client. "We'd all worked together on prior projects over the years—enough, we assumed, to know one another's 'sweet spots,'" he told us. "Over time, though, I grew more and more frustrated that two of my partners kept adding bits of regulatory advice to the pitch document—that's why I was on the team! I was handling nearly the exact same issue for a current client. I felt undermined, and the more they tried to sideline me, the more cantankerous I got." A few days before the client meeting, the group talked it out and discovered that Sherif had been honing his specialist expertise on projects the others hadn't been part of. They simply didn't realize what he had to offer. "We'd all been running in so many directions at the same time that our individual knowledge was changing quickly," he says. "No wonder we had friction."

Skills mapping could have prevented this. It also streamlines communication (no need to "reply all" if you know who's actually responsible for an issue). And it equips members to hold one another accountable for high-quality, on-time delivery, which is otherwise tricky when people are frequently coming and going. Creating the expectation of peer accountability relieves you as the team leader from some of that day-to-day oversight, freeing you up to scan the environment for potential shocks from other teams, for example, or to handle some of the inevitable negotiations about shared resources.

Manage time across teams. As you form a team, explicitly talk about everyone's competing priorities up front. By preemptively identifying crunch periods across projects, you can revamp deadlines or plan on spending more hands-on time yourself at certain points. Making the topic "discussable" so that people won't feel guilty about conflicts allows the team to openly and productively handle these issues when they come up later.

Establishing the right rhythm of meetings will make it easier to manage time across teams and address competing priorities. At the outset, you'll want to schedule several full-team meetings at critical junctures. (Research shows, for instance, that the halfway point in any project is a vital moment for a check-in, because that's when people shift into a higher gear, acutely aware that their time is limited.) Make attendance truly mandatory, and ensure it by giving each team member a piece of the meetings to run—even if it's just for 10 minutes. Check in early to see that all members have cleared meeting dates with their other teams. Ideally, the organizational culture will support formal check-in meetings as a high priority. If not, you may need to coordinate with other team leaders before putting a schedule together.

When you plan other team meetings, invite exactly who's needed and no one else, to minimize scheduling conflicts with other teams. Most of the time, you won't need everyone. Meet in subteams whenever possible. Don't forget to leverage technology: Instead of using precious live meeting time for updates, send a three-line email or keep an online dashboard updated so that people can track progress as needed. Although technology doesn't replace face-to-face interaction, it can tide you over when a full meeting is too costly. And be creative: Younger team members are more likely to watch a 30-second video update than to read a two-page memo. Brief, spontaneous check-ins with team members over Skype or FaceTime can keep you updated on their competing deadlines; this visual interaction makes it more likely that you'll pick up cues about their stress and motivation levels, too.

Create a learning environment. Learning makes work feel more meaningful, and it's supposed to be a major benefit of multiteaming—but it often gets crowded out by time pressures. There are other obstacles as well: Even if you've worked to build trust and personal connections, it's harder for multiteamers to give effective feedback than it is for dedicated team members, because people whose time is divided among several projects are less likely to regularly observe their teammates' actions or to be present at a time that "feels right" to offer critiques. Members who see only a small slice of a project may lack the context to fully understand what kind of feedback is appropriate. They also tend to focus on short-term tasks and to communicate with one another only when required.

    Carrie, for example, was promoted to run the development office of a major metropolitan hospital, and her new 20-person staff was splitting its time among dozens of projects each week. After six months she realized, "We were all living in a feedback desert. I literally hadn't had a single comment in half a year about how I could do my job better, despite clear examples of projects that hadn't lived up to expectations." To change the tone, she modeled seeking input and responding to it constructively. "Doing so day in and day out, I started to create an environment where people shared their concerns to get help as soon as they needed it," she says. "Over time, it felt safe enough to put in more-formal processes to review projects and allow everyone to learn from errors without fear of retribution or blame."

You can also designate team members from different functions or offices to colead parts of the project so that they benefit from greater cross-contact; a formal assignment makes it more likely that they'll devote time to learning from each other. Similarly, pair a highly experienced team member with someone more junior and help them understand what both can gain from the exchange—it's not just one-way learning flowing down to the junior person.

Foster curiosity by posing "What if . . .?" questions when it's likely that different members' backgrounds will provide new insights. If you get a question that you know another member could answer more fully, given his or her experience, redirect the asker and prompt the expert to do a bit of tutoring.

Boost motivation. On traditional, fixed teams, a strong sense of cohesion and group identity motivates members. But leaders in multiteaming environments need to leverage more of an exchange relationship. The ability to get jazzed about a project naturally flags when members spend only a small amount of time on it. Their inner accountant asks, "If I'll get only 10% of the credit, how much time and effort should I devote to this?" Figure out what your ten-percenters really value and frame the work in terms of those rewards. For example, if you have a Millennial who is eager to develop transferable skills, you might occasionally take time during meetings to have team members

Goals of multiteaming (and the challenges that can undermine them)

Goals for teams	Challenges
Cost savings, because team members whose expertise is not required at the moment can bill their downtime to other projects	Weakened relationships and coherence within teams and projects
Process improvements, as a result of importing best practices and insights through shared members	Stress and burnout, particularly when members end up with assignments that exceed 100% time commitment
	Interteam coordination costs so that schedules of projects with shared members don't collide
	Rocky transitions as members switch between tasks where their contributions are defined relative to other members' skills, adjust to different roles (boss on one team but subordinate on another), and learn new team contexts with unfamiliar routines, symbols, jokes, expectations, tolerance for ambiguity, and so on
	Reduced learning, because members lack time together to share knowledge and ideas
	Reduced motivation, because members have a small percentage of their time dedicated to any given project

Goals for organizations	Challenges
The capacity to solve complex problems with members who have deep, specialized knowledge	Politics and tensions over shared human resources
Improved resource utilization across projects (no one is dedicated to a project that needs only 5% of his or her time)	Coordination costs of aligning timelines of projects even when they are not linked by content or workflow
Increased knowledge transfer and learning through shared membership	Weakened identification with the organization if people feel commoditized
	Increased risk as shocks affecting one team may pull shared members off other projects

share and learn something new, or hold a workshop at the end of the project in which members cross-train.

Remember, too, that a sense of fairness drives many behaviors. If people feel they are pulling their weight while others slack off, they quickly become demotivated. When team members are tugged in many directions, it's often difficult for each one to recognize and appreciate how hard the others are working. As the leader, keep publicly acknowledging various members' contributions so that they become visible to the whole team, spawning a greater awareness of the collective efforts.

Like Christine, the frustrated leader of the Analytix software team, you might be feeling the strain of sharing valuable talent with other teams. Before you reach the breaking point, take these steps to clarify and manage your interdependency with other teams. They will help you avoid conflicts when that's possible, defuse them when it's not, and set an example of better collaboration with other team leaders—peers who face the same challenges you do.

Priorities for organizational leaders

If you're leading an organization where multiteaming is prevalent, you'll need to keep a close eye on how—and how many—members are shared across teams. We've found that you can reduce organizational risk and boost innovation by following these steps:

Map and analyze human capital interdependence. Patterns of team overlap range from highly concentrated (a large proportion of members are shared by just a few teams) to highly dispersed (the sharing is spread out across many teams).

Who's feeling the pain?

At one professional services firm, the employees most squeezed by multiteaming were midtenure associates—they helped with more and more projects as they gained experience. But the more senior people became, the more likely they were to lead many projects at the same time.

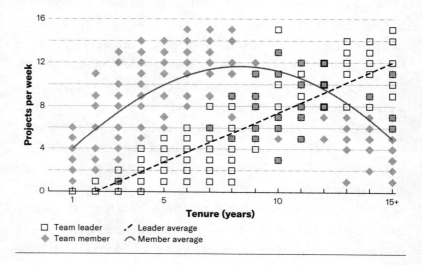

Each pattern has its own implications for risk management. When a surprise problem jolts one team, the cry "All hands on deck" pulls shared members off their other teams—with disproportionately large effects on teams that have a concentrated overlap in members. When the overlap is more dispersed, the shock will be felt by more teams but to a lesser extent by each one.

There are implications for knowledge transfer as well. Best practices travel from one project to the next as team members share what's working—and what isn't—on their other projects. Highly concentrated overlap makes it easier to spread ideas from one team to another; highly dispersed overlap makes it easier to spread them to more teams.

Keep an accurate map of the links among teams in your organization through periodic updates from managers and team members. The frequency of these check-ins will depend on the life cycles of your teams. You'll need them more often if teams and assignments change week to week, less often if you've got yearlong projects with stable membership. This bird's-eye view will help you see which teams fail to pick up on new trends because they're too isolated, for instance, and which are so tightly interconnected that they aren't mitigating the risks of their shared membership.

The question we get most often about mapping interdependence is "What's the right amount?" Unfortunately, there's no magic answer—either for overlap between teams or for the number of teams per individual. Both targets depend highly on context. When teams are very similar in their tasks and culture, transitioning between them is relatively easy, so you can have a large amount of overlap and members can be on more of them. Transitioning across teams with very different tasks or cultures should be kept to a minimum, however—it's a bigger, costlier shift. Interestingly, the reverse holds true when workloads differ across teams, because members aren't in high demand from all teams at the same time (they aren't as susceptible to burnout as, say, tax advisers in April are).

Once you've done all this analysis, it's time to address the shortcomings you've uncovered—which brings us to the next two steps.

Promote knowledge flows. Pay close attention to teams that share few or no members with others—whether that's by design or by accident. These "islands" will require help staying informed about what's working elsewhere in the organization, sharing their knowledge and ideas, and deciding who would be the best resource to apply to a given task.

Your goal here is to establish knowledge transfer as a cultural norm, which involves getting employees to recognize that everyone wins when they take the time to share insights across projects. As with any cultural shift, it's important to lead by example and to reward those who follow suit. That's simple to say—but not so simple to do. To make it easier, highlight the benefits of sharing, and provide processes and technology to facilitate it, such as brown-bag lunches and online forums. One tech firm we worked with made a point of celebrating project breakthroughs that were attributed to transferred best practices. R&D teams at a manufacturing company shared monthly testimonials from individuals who had gained new insights through cross-staffing. In both cases the objective was to make the benefits of knowledge transfer clear—and to counter the ever-present pressure for people to keep their heads down and focus on immediate tasks.

Buffer against shocks. How can you prevent shocks in one team from being transmitted to others? Often you can't—but knowing how teams are connected through shared membership allows you to anticipate *where* some shocks may be transferred and to design small amounts of slack into the system to absorb them. This doesn't mean having people sit around twiddling their thumbs just in case. Rather, you're enabling them to shift their attention when needed. One engineering firm we worked with had identified several skilled "firefighters" and assigned them to long-term projects that wouldn't suffer if they had to address urgent problems elsewhere. This had the added benefit of providing those individuals with exciting challenges that were a welcome change of pace from their day-to-day work.

It takes a critical eye and a clear set of strategic priorities to determine which projects can be disrupted and which can't. Sometimes it makes sense to give certain projects "protected" status, exempting members of those teams from answering others' firefighting calls. Overall, the idea is to be responsive to immediate problems without sacrificing teams' ongoing needs. Of course, even if you've built slack into team design, you may occasionally have to jump in with extra resources to save critical projects that take a hit. But your other teams will feel less pain when you do.

None of this is easy. You may need to work with HR or IT to establish processes or systems that will allow you to track multiteaming more accurately across the organization. You may even need to create a new role to define and coordinate these efforts effectively. And people may resist the increased oversight—it can feel like micromanagement to team leaders and members who are accustomed to having freer rein, particularly in entrepreneurial cultures. Still, in the end such investments are worthwhile; it's actually more costly to allow the trade-offs of multiteaming to go unchecked. If you're open about the problems you're trying to solve with all this transparency, people are less likely to feel surveilled or constrained by it and more likely to see the upside.

. . .

Nearly every knowledge worker these days is a member of multiple concurrent teams. Together, organizational and team leaders can make the most of that trend by creating an environment where multiteamers will thrive. Some of this involves managing interdependence risks, articulating and navigating groups' competing priorities, and removing obstacles to strategic coordination across groups. And some entails building stronger connections and greater trust among people who spend only a small fraction of their time together.

All around, it's a significant investment of time and effort. But organizations pay a much higher price when they neglect the costs of multiteaming in hot pursuit of its benefits.

Originally published in September–October 2017. Reprint R1705C

6

Global Teams That Work

by Tsedal Neeley

To succeed in the global economy today, more and more companies are relying on a geographically dispersed workforce. They build teams that offer the best functional expertise from around the world, combined with deep, local knowledge of the most promising markets. They draw on the benefits of international diversity, bringing together people from many cultures with varied work experiences and different perspectives on strategic and organizational challenges. All this helps multinational companies compete in the current business environment.

But managers who actually lead global teams are up against stiff challenges. Creating successful work groups is hard enough when everyone is local and people share the same office space. But when team members come from different countries and functional backgrounds and are working in different locations, communication can rapidly deteriorate, misunderstanding can ensue, and cooperation can degenerate into distrust.

Preventing this vicious dynamic from taking place has been a focus of my research, teaching, and consulting for more than 15 years. I have conducted dozens of studies and heard from countless executives and managers about misunderstandings within the global teams they have joined or led, sometimes with costly consequences. But I have also encountered teams that have produced remarkable innovations, creating millions of dollars in value for their customers and shareholders.

One basic difference between global teams that work and those that don't lies in the level of social distance—the degree of emotional connection among team members. When people on a team all work in the same place, the level of social distance is usually low. Even if they come from different backgrounds, people can interact formally and informally, align, and build trust. They arrive at a common understanding of what certain behaviors mean, and they feel close and congenial, which fosters good teamwork. Coworkers who are geographically separated, however, can't easily connect and align, so they experience high levels of social distance and struggle to develop effective interactions. Mitigating social distance therefore becomes the primary management challenge for the global team leader.

To help in this task, I have developed and tested a framework for identifying and successfully managing social distance. It is called the SPLIT framework, reflecting its five components: structure, process, language, identity, and technology—each of which can be a source of social distance. In the following pages I explain how each can lead to team dysfunction and describe how smart leaders can fix problems that occur—or prevent them from happening in the first place.

Idea in Brief

The Problem
When teams consist of people from different cultures working apart from one another in different locations, social distance—or a lack of emotional connection—can cause miscommunication, misunderstanding, and distrust.

The Solution
The leaders of global teams can improve the workings of their groups by using the author's SPLIT framework to identify and address five sources of social distance: structure, process, language, identity, and technology.

Structure and the Perception of Power

In the context of global teams, the structural factors determining social distance are the location and number of sites where team members are based and the number of employees who work at each site.

The fundamental issue here is the perception of power. If most team members are located in Germany, for instance, with two or three in the United States and in South Africa, there may be a sense that the German members have more power. This imbalance sets up a negative dynamic. People in the larger (majority) group may feel resentment toward the minority group, believing that the latter will try to get away with contributing less than its fair share. Meanwhile, those in the minority group may believe that the majority is usurping what little power and voice they have.

The situation is exacerbated when the leader is at the site with the most people or the one closest to company headquarters: Team members at that site tend to ignore the needs and contributions of their colleagues at other locations. This dynamic can occur even when everyone is in the same country: The five people working in, say, Beijing may have a strong allegiance to one another and a habit of shutting out their two colleagues in Shanghai.

When geographically dispersed team members perceive a power imbalance, they often come to feel that there are in-groups and out-groups. Consider the case of a global marketing team for a U.S.-based multinational pharmaceutical company. The leader and the core strategy group for the Americas worked in the company's Boston-area headquarters. A smaller group in London and a single individual in Moscow focused on the markets in Europe. Three other team members, who split their time between Singapore and Tokyo, were responsible for strategy in Asia. The way that each group perceived its situation is illustrated in the exhibit below.

To correct perceived power imbalances between different groups, a leader needs to get three key messages across:

Who we are

The team is a single entity, even though individual members may be very different from one another. The leader should encourage sensitivity to differences but look for ways to bridge them and build unity. Tariq, a 33-year-old rising star in a global firm, was assigned to lead a 68-person division whose members hailed from 27 countries, spoke 18 languages, and ranged in age from 22 to 61. During the two years before he took charge, the group's performance had been in a precipitous decline and employee satisfaction had plunged. Tariq saw that the team had fractured into subgroups according to location and language. To

> ## Views from a Dispersed Team
>
> The marketing team of a multinational pharmaceutical company had 17 members in different locations. Each group, depending on size and proximity to the leader in Boston, saw the power structure differently.
>
> *Moscow, one person*
> "I am all on my own here and at the mercy of the Boston group. I need to make sure that my boss has my back."
>
> *Singapore/Tokyo, three people*
> "Our opinions are often ignored, It's so difficult to find a good time to exchange ideas, and even if we do manage to connect, we can't get a word in edgewise."
>
> *London, five people*
> "We represent the most challenging regions in terms of diversity and institutional hurdles. The Boston team doesn't really understand our markets."
>
> *Boston, eight people*
> "We do the important work and have easy access to the boss."

bring people back together, he introduced a team motto ("We are different yet one"), created opportunities for employees to talk about their cultures, and instituted a zero-tolerance policy for displays of cultural insensitivity.

What we do

It's important to remind team members that they share a common purpose and to direct their energy toward business-unit or corporate goals. The leader should periodically highlight how everyone's work fits into the company's overall strategy and advances its position in the market. For instance, during a weekly conference call, a global team leader might review the group's performance relative to company objectives. She might also discuss the level of collective focus and sharpness the team needs in order to fend off competitors.

I am there for you

Team members located far from the leader require frequent contact with him or her. A brief phone call or email can make all the difference in conveying that their contributions matter. For instance, one manager in Dallas, Texas, inherited a large group in India as part of an acquisition. He made it a point to involve those employees in important decisions, contact them frequently to discuss ongoing projects, and thank them for good work. He even called team members personally to give them their birthdays off. His team appreciated his attention and became more cohesive as a result.

Process and the Importance of Empathy

It almost goes without saying that empathy helps reduce social distance. If colleagues can talk informally around a watercooler—whether about work or about personal matters—they are more likely to develop an empathy that helps them interact productively in more-formal contexts. Because geographically dispersed team members lack regular face time, they are less likely to have a sense of mutual understanding. To foster this, global team leaders need to make sure they build the following "deliberate moments" into the process for meeting virtually:

Feedback on routine interactions

Members of global teams may unwittingly send the wrong signals with their everyday behavior. Julie, a French chemical engineer, and her teammates in Marseille checked and responded to emails only first thing in the morning, to ensure an uninterrupted workday. They had no idea that this practice was routinely adding an overnight delay to correspondence with their American colleagues and contributing to mistrust. It was not until Julie visited the team's offices in California that the French group realized there was a problem. Of course, face-to-face visits are not the only way to acquire such learning. Remote team members can also use the phone, email, or even videoconferencing to check in with one another and ask how the collaboration is going. The point is that leaders and members of global teams must actively elicit this kind of "reflected knowledge," or awareness of how others see them.

Unstructured time

Think back to your last face-to-face meeting. During the first few minutes before the official discussion began, what was the atmosphere like? Were people comparing notes on the weather, their kids, that new restaurant in town? Unstructured communication like this is positive, because it allows for the organic unfolding of processes that must occur in all business dealings—sharing knowledge, coordinating and monitoring interactions, and building relationships. Even when people are spread all over the world, small talk is still a powerful way to promote trust. So when planning your team's call-in meetings, factor in five minutes for light conversation before business gets underway. Especially during the first meetings, take the lead in initiating informal discussions about work and nonwork matters that allow team members to

Rules of Engagement for Team Meetings

All team members should be guided by these three rules to ensure that influence on decisions is not dictated by fluency in the company's lingua franca.

Fluent speakers: Dial down dominance

- Slow down the pace and use familiar language (e.g., fewer idioms).
- Refrain from dominating the conversation.
- Ask: "Do you understand what I am saying?"
- Listen actively

Less fluent speakers: Dial up engagement

- Resist withdrawal or other avoidance behaviors.
- Refrain from reverting to your native language.
- Ask: "Do you understand what I am saying?"
- If you don't understand others, ask them to repeat or explain.

Team leaders: Balance for inclusion

- Monitor participants and strive to balance their speaking and listening.
- Actively draw contributions from all team members.
- Solicit participation from less fluent speakers in particular.
- Be prepared to define and interpret content.

get to know their distant counterparts. In particular, encourage people to be open about constraints they face outside the project, even if those aren't directly linked to the matter at hand.

Time to disagree

Leaders should encourage disagreement both about the team's tasks and about the process by which the tasks get done. The challenge, of course, is to take the heat out of the debate. Framing meetings as brainstorming opportunities lowers the risk that people will feel pressed to choose between sides. Instead, they will see an invitation to evaluate agenda items and contribute their ideas. As the leader, model the act of questioning to get to the heart of things. Solicit each team member's views on each topic you discuss, starting with those who have the least status or experience with the group so that they don't feel intimidated by others' comments. This may initially seem like a waste of time, but if you seek opinions up front, you may make better decisions and get buy-in from more people.

A software developer in Istanbul kept silent in a team meeting in order to avoid conflict, even though he questioned his colleagues' design of a particular feature. He had good reasons to oppose their decision, but his team leader did not brook disagreement, and the developer did not want to damage his own position. However, four weeks into the project, the team ran into the very problems that the developer had seen coming.

Language and the Fluency Gap

Good communication among coworkers drives effective knowledge sharing, decision making, coordination, and, ultimately, performance results (see also "What's Your Language Strategy?"

by Tsedal Neeley and Robert Steven Kaplan, HBR, September 2014). But in global teams, varying levels of fluency with the chosen common language are inevitable—and likely to heighten social distance. The team members who can communicate best in the organization's lingua franca (usually English) often exert the most influence, while those who are less fluent often become inhibited and withdraw. Mitigating these effects typically involves insisting that all team members respect three rules for communicating in meetings:

Dial down dominance

Strong speakers must agree to slow down their speaking pace and use fewer idioms, slang terms, and esoteric cultural references when addressing the group. They should limit the number of comments they make within a set time frame, depending on the pace of the meeting and the subject matter. They should actively seek confirmation that they've been understood, and they should practice active listening by rephrasing others' statements for clarification or emphasis.

Dial up engagement

Less fluent speakers should monitor the frequency of their responses in meetings to ensure that they are contributing. In some cases, it's even worth asking them to set goals for the number of comments they make within a given period. Don't let them use their own language and have a teammate translate, because that can alienate others. As with fluent speakers, team members who are less proficient in the language must always confirm that they have been understood. Encourage them to routinely ask if others are following them. Similarly, when listening, they should be empowered to say they have not understood something. It can be tough for nonnative speakers to make this leap, yet doing so keeps them from being marginalized.

Balance participation to ensure inclusion

Getting commitments to good speaking behavior is the easy part; making the behavior happen will require active management. Global team leaders must keep track of who is and isn't contributing and deliberately solicit participation from less fluent speakers. Sometimes it may also be necessary to get dominant-language speakers to dial down to ensure that the proposals and perspectives of less fluent speakers are heard.

The leader of a global team based in Dubai required all his reports to post the three communication rules in their cubicles. Soon he noted that one heavily accented European team member began contributing to discussions for the first time since joining the group 17 months earlier. The rules had given this person the license, opportunity, and responsibility to speak up. As a leader, you could try the same tactics with your own team, distributing copies of the exhibit "Rules of Engagement for Team Meetings."

Identity and the Mismatch of Perceptions

Global teams work most smoothly when members "get" where their colleagues are coming from. However, deciphering someone's identity and finding ways to relate is far from simple. People define themselves in terms of a multitude of variables—age, gender, nationality, ethnicity, religion, occupation, political ties, and so forth. And although behavior can be revealing, particular behaviors may signify different things depending on the individual's identity. For example, someone in North America who looks you squarely in the eye may project confidence and honesty, but in other parts of the world, direct eye contact might be perceived as rude or threatening. Misunderstandings such as this are a major source of social distance and distrust, and global team leaders have to raise everyone's awareness of them. This involves mutual learning and teaching.

Learning from one another

When adapting to a new cultural environment, a savvy leader will avoid making assumptions about what behaviors mean. Take a step back, watch, and listen. In America, someone who says, "Yes, I can do this" likely means she is willing and able to do what you asked. In India, however, the same statement may simply signal that she wants to try—not that she's confident of success. Before drawing conclusions, therefore, ask a lot of questions. In the example just described, you might probe to see if the team member anticipates any challenges or needs additional resources. Asking for this information may yield greater insight into how the person truly feels about accomplishing the task.

The give-and-take of asking questions and providing answers establishes two-way communication between the leader and team members. And if a leader regularly solicits input, acting as a student rather than an expert with hidden knowledge, he empowers others on the team, leading them to participate more willingly and effectively. A non-Mandarin-speaking manager in China relied heavily on his local staff during meetings with clients in order to better understand clients' perceptions of the interactions and to gauge the appropriateness of his own behavior. His team members began to see themselves as essential to the development of client relationships and felt valued, which motivated them to perform at even higher levels.

In this model, everyone is a teacher and a learner, which enables people to step out of their traditional roles. Team members take on more responsibility for the development of the team as a whole. Leaders learn to see themselves as unfinished and are thus more likely to adjust their style to reflect the team's needs. They instruct but they also facilitate, helping team members to parse their observations and understand one another's true identities.

A case in point

Consider the experience of Daniel, the leader of a recently formed multinational team spread over four continents. During a conference call, he asked people to discuss a particular strategy for reaching a new market in a challenging location. This was the first time he had raised a topic on which there was a range of opinion.

Daniel observed that Theo, a member of the Israeli team, regularly interrupted Angela, a member of the Buenos Aires team, and their ideas were at odds. Although tempted to jump in and play referee, Daniel held back. To his surprise, neither Theo nor Angela got frustrated. They went back and forth, bolstering their positions by referencing typical business practices and outcomes in their respective countries, but they stayed committed to reaching a group consensus.

At the meeting's end, Daniel shared his observations with the team, addressing not only the content of the discussion, but also the manner in which it took place. "Theo and Angela," he said, "when you began to hash out your ideas, I was concerned that both of you might have felt you weren't being heard or weren't getting a chance to fully express your thoughts. But now you both seem satisfied that you were able to make your arguments, articulate cultural perspectives, and help us decide on our next steps. Is that true?"

Theo and Angela affirmed Daniel's observations and provided an additional contextual detail: Six months earlier they had worked together on another project—an experience that allowed them to establish their own style of relating to each other. Their ability to acknowledge and navigate their cultural differences was beneficial to everyone on the team. Not only did it help move their work forward, but it showed that conflict does not have to create social distance. And Daniel gained more information about Theo and Angela, which would help him manage the team more effectively in the future.

Technology and the Connection Challenge

The modes of communication used by global teams must be carefully considered, because the technologies can both reduce and increase social distance. Videoconferencing, for instance, allows rich communication in which both context and emotion can be perceived. Email offers greater ease and efficiency but lacks contextual cues. In making decisions about which technology to use, a leader must ask the following:

Should communication be instant?

Teleconferencing and videoconferencing enable real-time (instant) conversations. Email and certain social media formats require users to wait for the other party to respond. Choosing between instant and delayed forms of communication can be especially challenging for global teams. For example, when a team spans multiple time zones, a telephone call may not be convenient for everyone. The Japanese team leader of a U.S.-based multinational put it this way: "I have three or four days per week when I have a conference call with global executives. In most cases, it starts at 9:00 or 10:00 in the night. If we can take the conference call in the daytime, it's much easier for me. But we are in the Far East, and headquarters is in the United States, so we have to make the best of it."

Instant technologies are valuable when leaders need to persuade others to adopt their viewpoint. But if they simply want to share information, then delayed methods such as email are simpler, more efficient, and less disruptive to people's lives. Leaders must also consider the team's interpersonal dynamics. If the team has a history of conflict, technology choices that limit the opportunities for real-time emotional exchanges may yield the best results.

In general, the evidence suggests that most companies overrely on delayed communication. A recent Forrester survey of nearly 10,000 information workers in 17 countries showed that 94% of employees report using email, but only 33% ever participate in desktop videoconferencing (with apps such as Skype and Viber), and a mere 25% use room-based videoconferencing. These numbers will surely change over time, as the tools evolve and users become more comfortable with them, but leaders need to choose their format carefully: instant or delayed.

Do I need to reinforce the message?

Savvy leaders will communicate through multiple platforms to ensure that messages are understood and remembered. For example, if a manager electronically assigns one of her team members a task by entering notes into a daily work log, she may then follow up with a text or a face-to-face chat to ensure that the team member saw the request and recognized its urgency.

Redundant communication is also effective for leaders who are concerned about convincing others that their message is important. Greg, for instance, a project manager in a medical devices organization, found that his team was falling behind on the development of a product. He called an emergency meeting to discuss the issues and explain new corporate protocols for releasing new products, which he felt would bring the project back on track.

During this initial meeting, he listened to people's concerns and addressed their questions in real time. Although he felt he had communicated his position clearly and obtained the necessary verbal buy-in, he followed up the meeting by sending a carefully drafted email to all the attendees, reiterating the agreed-upon changes and asking for everyone's electronic sign-off. This redundant communication helped reinforce acceptance of his ideas and increased the likelihood that his colleagues would actually implement the new protocols.

Am I leading by example?

Team members very quickly pick up on the leader's personal preferences regarding communication technology. A leader who wants to encourage people to videoconference should communicate this way herself. If she wants employees to pick up the phone and speak to one another, she had better be a frequent user of the phone. And if she wants team members to respond quickly to emails, she needs to set the example.

. . .

Flexibility and appreciation for diversity are at the heart of managing a global team. Leaders must expect problems and patterns to change or repeat themselves as teams shift, disband, and regroup. But there is at least one constant: To manage social distance effectively and maximize the talents and engagement of team members, leaders must stay attentive to all five of the SPLIT dimensions. Decisions about *structure* create opportunities for good *process*, which can mitigate difficulties caused by *language* differences and *identity* issues. If leaders act on these fronts, while marshaling *technology* to improve communication among geographically dispersed colleagues, social distance is sure to shrink, not expand. When that happens, teams can become truly representative of the "global village"—not just because of their international makeup, but also because their members feel mutual trust and a sense of kinship. They can then embrace and practice the kind of innovative, respectful, and groundbreaking interactions that drive the best ideas forward.

Originally published in October 2015. Reprint R1510D

QUICK READ

Four Types of Team Conflict—and How to Resolve Them

by Randall S. Peterson, Priti Pradhan Shah, Amanda J. Ferguson, and Stephen L. Jones

If you have ever managed a team or worked on one, you know that conflict within a team is as inevitable as it is distracting. Many managers avoid dealing with conflict in their team where possible, hoping reasonable people can work it out. Despite this, research shows that managers spend upward of 20% of their time, on average, managing conflict.[1]

Consider Barbara, a senior executive who shared a memorable story with us about calling a special team meeting at the end of a particularly brutal day of bad news. Her planned purpose for the meeting was to agree on actions to take in hopes of getting the team back on track. What she got in the meeting, unfortunately, was a lot of team members blaming each other and defending their own individual actions. Within 10 minutes, she knew she needed to change tactics or the meeting would spiral out of control.

Over the past three decades, we have studied thousands of team conflicts—from management teams in multinational companies like Barbara's to assembly teams in factories in China to MBAs at top business schools. We have asked managers to share their stories of team conflict, surveyed executives, and observed conflict as it unfolds in boardrooms. Our aim has been to understand what team conflict looks like and how it evolves over time so that we can help managers improve team performance.[2]

Despite all the differences in culture and content, we have identified four common patterns that cover virtually all team conflicts. Our work also shows that when managers take a proactive role in resolving conflict that respects the interests of the whole team, the outcomes can actually be positive and result in increased trust and better decisions that are more likely to be effectively implemented. Here are the patterns of conflict we identified along with how to manage each one.

The Solo Dissenter: Conflict Surrounds One Individual

Sometimes team conflict surrounds one individual on a team. This person may be the odd one out who is difficult to get along with or is not motivated to engage with other team members. Or this person could be the devil's advocate who pushes the team, trying to get others to consider different ways of working when the team is too comfortable. Whatever the reason, it is easy to see that the tension or debate that exists in the team is attributable to this one person. Conflict due to one individual is quite common, occurring in about 20% to 25% of team conflicts.[3]

If your team experiences this kind of conflict, make sure that the members do not gang up on the individual. It's easy to make

Idea in Brief

The Problem
Managers spend more than 20% of their time managing team conflict but often fail to prevent its worst effects, hoping the people involved will just work things out.

Why It Matters
When conflict is resolved in a way that respects the interests of the whole team, the outcomes can be positive and result in increased trust and better decisions that are more likely to be effectively implemented.

The Solution
Managers must take a more proactive role. The first step is identifying which of four common types of conflict is plaguing the team so you can tailor your efforts at resolution based on the number of people involved. Are you dealing with a **solo dissenter**, a **boxing match** between two people, two subgroups or **warring factions**, or a whole-team disagreement in which everyone is playing **the blame game**?

---

this person a scapegoat for all things negative that plague the team or to shut them down by invoking "majority rules" and moving on quickly from the argument, but this is a mistake. It doesn't allow you to uncover potential underlying problems, like whether this person is experiencing personal challenges or whether their team role is unclear or unmotivating. Perspective-taking is a better approach and can often ease tensions. You can model this approach in team meetings for members to see. Ask the solo dissenter sincere questions to understand their unique perspective and build empathy toward them, while simultaneously creating new insights for your team. Research shows that when people are exposed to different points of view, it makes them more likely to think divergently, and that increases their capacity to learn and understand the problems more deeply.[4]

Avoid subjecting everyone to team building if you're dealing with a solo dissenter. It is likely to annoy the majority of team members who know they are not the problem, and it does not address the fundamental issue. Instead, you as team leader or another member of the team could intervene with this person one-on-one. Being open to learning more, expressing understanding, and coaching this person can go a long way to building bridges. So, if Barbara discovers that the team's friction is primarily coming from one individual, she should have a conversation with that person and not involve the whole team.

The Boxing Match: Two People Within a Team Disagree

The most common pattern of conflict in teams is when two people disagree, comprising approximately 35% of team conflict. You may assume that this pattern will escalate to include others over time, but the evidence suggests otherwise. Most people tend to avoid taking sides when there is a dyadic conflict embedded within a group, making it most likely that the duo will continue to box until one is knocked out, or a referee steps in to mediate.

Dyadic conflict can be relationship-based, for example, when two people have a history of animosity toward one another. If that is the case, tread carefully when trying to resolve it. It is possible that mediation may help, where meeting with each individual separately and then together helps them vent their feelings and perspectives. Make these sessions separate from the team and private. Do not let mediation be a drama for the rest of the team to watch; indeed, some members may be unaware that the conflict exists. Alternatively, consider whether these two need to be on the same team, and if so, if there is a way to redesign workflows to minimize their need to interact. For example, if Barbara discovers that her team's conflict is primarily dyadic and centered on a dysfunctional relationship, she needs to find a way to separate the two parties.

If a team's conflict is dyadic but centered on the team's tasks, leaders should use a different strategy. If kept civil, this kind of disagreement will likely help the team perform better in the long run. And it often resolves naturally as the team coalesces around what actions to take. Small-scale debates about ideas, like those that happen between two people at the watercooler or while waiting for others to join a virtual meeting or between meetings, are essential for helping people informally vet their ideas. Like a "pair and share" exercise in classrooms, these grassroots debates give people the chance to disagree in a more intimate forum, reconsider their positions, and bring the best versions of their ideas to the team. We even found that teams with multiple pairs of people debating ideas outperform teams with a single dyadic conflict.

Given that task conflict can be advantageous to groups, a savvy leader might wonder whether they can unlock greater learning in the team by assigning a devil's advocate to create conflict between two or more members. Tempting as this sounds, it does not work. Studies show that artificial conflict or playing devil's advocate typically feels good as a process but does not produce the same psychological reaction as listening to authentically different points of view, nor does it translate into better decisions for the team. Rather than manufacturing artificial differences of opinion, the better strategy is to create a diverse team and take the time to allow and encourage genuine differences of opinion to emerge. These real differences of opinion have the actual potential to stimulate divergent thinking and improve team performance.

Warring Factions: Two Subgroups Within a Team Disagree

The third pattern of conflict occurs when two subgroups within the team are in opposition. Each subgroup may prefer a different team goal, project, or decision outcome. Most members are likely to be involved in this sort of conflict, taking one side or the other. This conflict accounts for about 20% to 25% of conflicts in teams.[5]

What makes this pattern of team conflict unique and dangerous, however, is that it creates approximately equal opposing sides with multiple members allied together on the two sides. With near-equal opposition in this us-versus-them scenario, no one will consider the other side's perspective, instead focusing on winning by digging in their heels on their preferred course of action. Strategies like voting will not work; even if one side comes up the winner, the other side typically feels ignored and will not likely support the implementation of the decision or execute it well.

Although counterintuitive, research suggests that you can break the deadlock by introducing additional ideas, alternatives, or goals to move past seemingly opposed courses of action.[6] Doing so allows subgroups to understand their underlying interests and make tradeoffs between issues that are more and less important, providing a more comprehensive solution that both sides can support. So, if Barbara's team conflict devolves into warring factions, she should probably bring in someone from the outside to challenge the group's thinking or present third, fourth, or fifth options.

The Blame Game: The Whole Team Disagrees

The prototypical picture of team conflict is of everyone arguing with one another, but, while this happens from time to time, it is relatively rare. Less than 15% of teams ever experience this pattern of outright conflict.[7]

This pattern of conflict can emerge early in a project when everyone has a different idea of what the team should do. But more often than not, whole-team conflict emerges in response to poor team performance and related feedback. Poor performance prompts members to assign blame to others who respond by shifting blame elsewhere, as Barbara experienced in the initial moments of her team meeting. As tempting as it is to assign blame for poor team performance to specific individuals, it usually generates more conflict than it resolves.

When whole-team conflict strikes, you need the team to come together in its best interests. That may mean better articulating the team's goal or vision or reaffirming the team's identity. In the case of a team failure, this most certainly means debriefing poor performance feedback by focusing on the collective and not identifying specific individuals. For example, leaders or members can articulate strategies that everyone on the team can improve or contribute to in a positive way—looking forward instead of rehashing who did what when.

Barbara was experiencing whole-team conflict. We advised her to shift the focus of conversation from looking at causes of the negative feedback to the need to work together to resolve the issues moving forward. The outcome was a shift in the room to a

The four patterns of team conflict

Each dot represents a member in a five-person team. Lines represent conflict between team members.

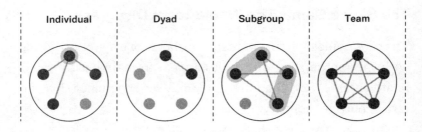

Source: Priti Pradhan Shah, Randall S. Peterson, and Amanda J. Ferguson, "Things Are Not Always What They Seem: The Origins and Evolution of Intragroup Conflict," *Administrative Science Quarterly* 66, no. 2 (October 10, 2020), https://journals.sagepub.com/doi/10.1177/0001839220965186.

more constructive tone and problem-solving that addressed the issues and led to improved team performance.

Tailoring Your Approach

Your team's conflict is likely as unique as the individuals involved and yet probably also fits into one of these four patterns. Knowing the pattern of your team's conflict gives you more information about the number of people involved, how they are involved, and where to focus your efforts when achieving positive outcomes from team conflict.

There are two key points managers and team leaders should remember. First, tackle conflict at its point of origin. Save those team-building retreats for conflict that involves all team members where whole-group unity is needed. Second, take care of conflict's "sides." When one side is represented by a minority (for example, one person), do not allow the majority to prematurely shut the other side down with a vote. When two equally balanced sides seem miles apart, add different options to spark creativity in integrating them. If you intervene smartly as close to the origin of the conflict as you can, you're more likely to stem its long-term consequences and improve team outcomes.

Adapted from "4 Common Types of Team Conflict—and How to Resolve Them" on hbr.org, May 7, 2024. Reprint H087IU

7

Why Employees Quit

by Ethan Bernstein, Michael B. Horn, and Bob Moesta

The so-called war for talent is still raging. But in that fight employers continue to rely on the same hiring and retention strategies they've been using for decades, even though those approaches aren't working: People may be enticed to stay a bit longer than they otherwise would have, but they still leave. So why do organizations persist with those strategies? Because they've been so focused on challenges such as tight labor markets, relentless cost-cutting pressures, and poaching by industry rivals that they haven't addressed a more fundamental problem: the widespread failure to provide gratifying work experiences. To stick around and keep giving their best, people need meaningful work; managers and colleagues who value, respect, and trust them; and opportunities to grow, excel, and advance in their careers.

Editor's note: Ethan Bernstein, Michael B. Horn, and Bob Moesta are the coauthors of Job Moves: 9 Steps for Making Progress in Your Career *(HarperCollins, 2024), from which this article is adapted.*

Although managers and their HR colleagues are beginning to understand that employee experience matters for hiring and retention, they haven't reached anything close to a consensus on what it should look like or how to provide it. Some workplaces invest heavily in wellness benefits and initiatives, with mixed results. Others try (and in many cases struggle) to create effective mentoring or learning and development programs—worthy endeavors but tough to get right if you haven't identified what employees want from them.

It's time to step way back from these related but typically uncoordinated efforts so that managers can see and address the larger issue of experience. Over the past 15 years we've collectively studied the behavioral patterns of more than a thousand job switchers at all levels and career stages—a racially diverse sample representing a wide range of roles and professions. In interviews, surveys, classroom discussions, consulting engagements, and coaching sessions, we've found again and again that employees who quit their jobs do so because they aren't making the progress they seek in their careers and lives.

By supporting people in their personal quests for progress—in ways that meet the organization's needs—managers can, our research suggests, create employee experiences that are mutually beneficial. In our qualitative dataset we found that career moves were driven primarily by four quests. We'll describe them here and discuss how managers can help employees on their journeys. But first let's take a closer look at the stakes for employers.

Attrition Is a Persistent, Costly Problem

Leaders can't reasonably blame their human capital troubles on the economic or competitive challenges of the day. Long

Idea in Brief

The Problem
Employers continue to rely on the same hiring and retention strategies they've been using for decades, but those approaches are failing. Employees are quitting their jobs in large numbers, generating significant costs for companies.

The Root Cause
Companies aren't providing sustainable work experiences that align with employees' personal quests for progress. Employees often feel stagnant, undervalued, and disconnected from meaningful work, which drives them to seek positions elsewhere.

The Solution
Managers should engage with employees early—soon after they've started their new jobs—to find out why they left their previous positions. In addition, managers should collaborate with HR to tailor roles to each individual's quest for progress.

---

before the Covid-19 pandemic, which saw the highest quit rates in U.S. history, employers complained that talented people were walking out the door with their knowledge, skills, and relationships. Those departures are expensive. Studies estimate that on average, the cost of losing an employee ranges from six to nine months' worth of that person's compensation. For technical and executive positions it can be as high as twice the employee's annual salary.

Despite copious employee surveys, pulse checks, and exit interviews, companies usually don't get to the bottom of why people quit. Departing employees may keep their reasons for leaving to themselves—out of fear that they'll burn bridges, for example, or out of a sense of futility. And we've often found in our coaching sessions that people aren't even clear themselves about their reasons for career moves until they sit down with a trusted coach, mentor, or friend who can help them understand what's really driving them. Most people don't do that. Instead they respond to job postings that grab their attention and switch jobs when they get a decent offer, hoping that things will improve—only to be dissatisfied down the line. Some switch again and again; many never find quite what they need.

The Forces That Compel Job Moves

The act of quitting (quiet or otherwise) is different for each person and driven by a variety of forces. Trying to retain employees without understanding what motivates them as individuals is like grabbing a flathead screwdriver out of your toolbox before checking whether the screw that needs attention is a Phillips head.

To make it easier for people to realize what led them to make a particular career move, we have identified the most common functional, social, and emotional forces that compel action (see the sidebar "The Push and Pull of a Job Switch"). In our research we explored a range of questions: What problems with a job's basic functions—assignments, projects, activities, tasks, and so on—can fuel a desire for change? To what extent can employees' met or unmet social needs drive career moves? How can employees' emotional needs—to feel energized, for example, rather than depleted—affect their willingness to trade in the familiar for the unknown?

In our conversations with job switchers, we heard that negative experiences (doing work that feels empty, for example, or disliking one's colleagues), along with changing life circumstances (such as moving or having kids), *pushed* individuals away from

The Push and Pull of a Job Switch

Current circumstances can push employees away, but people tend to stay put until they're also pulled toward something appealing. Among the job switchers we studied, these were the most common pushes and pulls precipitating a move:

I'm pushed when

- I don't respect or trust the people I work with.
- I feel that the work I'm doing has little or no impact on the company, the world, or my life.
- The way I'm managed day-to-day is wearing me down.
- My current company is struggling, and the end feels near.
- I end up with a new manager and feel like I'm starting over.
- I feel disrespected or not trusted.
- I've reached a personal milestone in my life.
- I've reached a milestone in my job or career.
- My work is dominating my life, and I sacrifice myself or my family to get things done.
- A trusted adviser, mentor, or previous boss guides me toward my next step.
- I am challenged beyond my ability, logic, or ethics.
- I feel unchallenged or bored in my current work.
- I can't see where to go or how to grow in my current organization (or progress will take too long or be too hard).
- I feel that I've been on my own, ignored, and unsupported at work for a long time.

(continued)

The Push and Pull of a Job Switch (continued)

I'm pulled when

- I can have more time to spend with others outside work.
- My values and beliefs will align with the company and the people I work with.
- My job will fit into my existing personal life.
- I can reset my life and start over.
- I can acquire the skills I need for a future job or career.
- I can be acknowledged, respected, and trusted to do great work.
- I can find an employer who values my experience and credentials.
- I and others will see my job as a step forward.
- I will have the freedom and flexibility to do my best work.
- I can be recognized for the impact of my work on other people and the business.
- I will have a supportive boss who guides me and provides constructive feedback.
- I can be part of a tight-knit team or community that I can count on.
- I can be challenged, grow, and learn on the job.
- I will be in a job that I know I can do and not feel at risk.
- I can support my growing personal responsibilities.
- I can have more time for me.

their old roles. The potential for positive experiences elsewhere *pulled* them toward something new. Those forces work together. Our findings square with research by the Wharton economist Katy Milkman, which shows that behavioral pushes become stronger when a new idea or solution pulls people toward something they aspire to. For example, a salesperson in our sample who felt micromanaged in his job stayed put until he was enticed by an offer that would allow him to take control over all aspects of the sales cycle.

To gather detailed information about prevalent pushes and pulls, we interviewed people not about their current circumstances—which might or might not prompt a career move—but about their most recent job switch.

Four Quests for Progress

Although pushes and pulls can work together in all sorts of ways, depending on life circumstances, we have found that they tend to cluster into four main quests. People who change jobs do so because they want to *get out* of their current situation, *regain control* of their work or lives, *regain alignment* between their work and their knowledge and capabilities, or *take the next step* in their careers. Job seekers often relate to more than one quest, but at any given time one takes priority over the others. (Our assessment at www.jobmoves.com can help the people you manage or mentor identify which quest they were on when they last left a job.)

Our research is rooted in the idea that just as customers "hire" products to do certain jobs for them, people can "hire" their next role to help them make the progress they want. Here we're drawing on the *jobs to be done* theory, which one of us (Bob) codeveloped with the innovation scholar Clayton Christensen to explain how makers of products can understand what customers hope to accomplish in a given circumstance (see "Know Your Customers' 'Jobs to Be Done,'" HBR, September 2016). Our interviews with job switchers uncovered the jobs to be done in their lives, which we call their *quests for progress*.

The quests have little to do with career progression as it's traditionally defined—a steady, linear ascent from junior to senior employee. Rather, progress zigzags according to what the individual wants most out of work and life at a particular time.

Let's look at each quest.

Get out. People who experience a classic fight-or-flight response are often being managed in a way that wears them down. They may feel stuck in a dead-end job or be in over their heads. Many face steep obstacles (such as a toxic culture, a role that's a bad fit, or an awful commute) that prevent them from putting their capabilities to good use. For whatever reason, they're strongly at odds with their work environment. They want a new job to rescue them from their current one.

Regain control. It's common for people to feel overwhelmed (or bored) at work, at home, or both. Some need a rebalance. Others simply want more predictability or flexibility in when and where they work. Unlike employees desperate to get out, control seekers aren't searching for the nearest escape hatch. They usually feel pretty good about their overall trajectory but not so good about the speed at which they are moving. They tend to hold off on switching until they find a job that will give them agency over their work environment.

Regain alignment. Most people seeking alignment feel a profound lack of respect at work and are hunting for a job where their skills and experience will be more fully utilized, appreciated, and acknowledged. Lacking such validation, they often have a dark outlook and fixate on the many ways their current role doesn't play to what they have to offer or what they wish to contribute. In their search for something new, they typically gravitate toward an environment where they believe they won't be underestimated or misunderstood.

Take the next step. After reaching a personal or professional milestone—such as completing schooling, achieving a development goal, or becoming empty nesters—job switchers are often eager to move forward in their careers. In many cases that means taking on more responsibility. Often driven by a desire to support themselves or their families, these individuals might want better healthcare benefits, a more comfortable living environment, the ability to pay for everyday basics or save for college, and so on. People on this quest—unlike those in the other three categories—aren't necessarily reacting to a bad situation. They're pursuing growth, so they may be willing to leap into a stretch role.

Armed with this knowledge about quests for progress and the forces behind them, you can work with your employees to tailor their experiences and even their roles to help them achieve the progress they seek. We recommend doing so in three ways: (1) Interview people long before they head for the exit. (2) Develop "shadow" job descriptions that speak to their—and your—real needs. (3) Huddle with HR to help employees make the progress they desire.

Interview Them Early On

As we noted earlier, exit interviews can be a bit of a joke. People usually assume it's too late to address why they are leaving—so they say safe things and move on.

We've found that it's more productive to interview employees about their previous roles soon after they've started something new. That's essentially what we did in our research. By closely examining the pushes and pulls that compelled each person's most recent job move, you can better understand what might motivate your employees to make another change soon—and, conversely, what might make them choose to stick around. You can frame these talks with employees as your way of identifying important features of their experience so that with their input you can create a workplace that they'll want to "rehire" each day. (See the sidebar "Why Did They Leave? An Interview Guide.")

In our mentoring and advising work, we regularly conduct these interviews to help people recognize underlying forces they aren't yet seeing on their own. To identify pushes and pulls, we suggest prodding for details, like an investigative journalist, while also approaching the conversation with empathy. Instead of weaving your assumptions into someone's story, ask lots of granular questions. For instance: *What was happening in your life when you first thought about switching jobs? What propelled you from passive to active looking? Throughout the job-switching process, what conversations did you have with people close to you? What worries and hopes did you discuss with them?*

We like to allow two hours for interviews: one to ask questions and listen, and one to debrief after a quick break. Take good notes so that you can easily refer back to details that may later seem important.

Why Did They Leave? An Interview Guide

Before interviewing people about their most recent job switch, set expectations. Tell them there's no need to prepare in advance. You're just going to chat. Nothing will be judged; everything will be kept confidential.

Then you can get started.

Liken the conversation to creating a documentary film about the person's career move.

With that frame in place, the process can be described along these lines:

Please tell me the details around when you started thinking about switching, when you made the decision, and when you actually came on board here. As you talk about a certain event or a realization you had, I might ask a bunch of questions, such as "Who was with you? What time of day was it? Where were you?" Think of this as capturing a close-up shot for this film so that we can get the specifics and the mood just right.

You don't need to use this exact language. Say what feels natural and put the other person at ease.

Ask for context about the job move.

Have the employee describe the previous job, what life was like then, and (briefly) what work and life are like now. Offer a prompt if one seems to be needed:

Just tell me whatever basics feel relevant, such as how long you were in your previous job, when you switched, and where you were living at the time.

Although you want details, you're not trying to create an exhaustive biography or act as an armchair psychologist. The objective is to understand the events leading up to the change.

(continued)

Why Did They Leave?
An Interview Guide (continued)

Let the employee talk uninterrupted for a bit.

You will probably hear all kinds of things about this most recent switch—which may or may not be relevant to the motivations behind it. Let all those thoughts come out at the beginning of the conversation. Then steer the interview to where you want it to go.

If you feel the employee's energy flagging, jump in.

Start focusing on the order of events. You might ask:

How did all this come about? Do you remember the first time you thought you might be ready to leave for another job?

To be fair, your employee might *not* remember—or a quick answer might not be accurate. Keep digging.

Follow up with highly specific questions.

For instance:

What was your day-to-day experience like the first year or two? What events led up to that shouting match between you and your coworker?

While working through the sequence of events, the employee may suddenly land on a key moment of realization.

Refer to other people in the employee's story by name.

If your interviewee mentions a difficult conversation with someone, for instance, use that person's name in your follow-up questions. Names trigger emotions and memories.

Empathize, but don't overdo it.

It's fine to show that you can relate (as in "Yeah, that's happened to me, too"), but you might come across as thinking you know everything if you interject too much. That tends to shut people down. Remain inquisitive.

Listen deeply.

When describing the circumstances surrounding the job switch, the employee might share an important insight such as "I was just so sick of missing my daughter's softball game yet again because of a fire drill at work and then having to explain to her why I missed it. It had to change." That's something solid you can build on. Play back what the person said—and then push a bit more.

Tease out deeper motivations by offering points of contrast.

For example, about those missed softball games you might ask:

How did you feel? Guilty and frustrated with yourself? Or annoyed by pressure from family members?

By offering two contrasting options, you can elicit an emotionally revealing response (quite possibly "Neither! It was this!") and gain greater insight.

To further explore what you learn, ask for more details.

How often were you missing family time for work? Were you missing other important things for the same reason? When did that start, and how often did it occur? When did it become a big problem?

Fill any holes.

When people use general language to describe events, the natural tendency is to nod along. Don't assume you understand. Again, contrast creates meaning. For example, if your employee ruled out another job offer because the manager didn't seem "nice," ask what that means:

Are managers nice when they are generous with praise? Or when they give you honest feedback without belittling you?

Both might be nice. But by holding up concrete examples, you can home in on what's really meant.

Change your line of inquiry if the employee starts just agreeing with you.

That can mean you're not getting the whole story. Revisit something you don't fully understand and probe for clarification.

(continued)

> ## Why Did They Leave?
> ## An Interview Guide (continued)
>
> *At the end of the story, replay what you heard start to finish.*
> Spell out the whole time line of events (this will be easier if you took copious notes) and give the employee space to correct things or add what you missed.

During the debrief look together at common pushes and pulls and discuss which ones are most relevant to this employee's latest job switch. Perhaps, for instance, the person was making too many sacrifices at home to get things done at work and didn't see a clear path for growth at the old company. Maybe the employee was drawn to the new role by the freedom and flexibility it affords and a desire to be part of a tight-knit community.

Once you've helped people clarify why they're here at your company, you can talk about what's still important to them, what may have changed since they started the current job, and what new forces they may encounter given what's going on in their lives now. If the path for growth in your organization is clear, great—but what's next? Which skills does the employee want to invest in? How might those be developed on the job, to avoid sacrificing family time? If community still matters a great deal, what can be learned from colleagues—and what can be taught in return—to deepen work relationships? How might those opportunities be folded into team or project assignments?

In this way you can work together on a career plan that serves both the employee's interests and those of the organization.

Joe Carver, who heads up leadership development at the Puget Sound Naval Shipyard, shows employees that he understands their past pushes by acting on the information they share with him. He told us that he often sits down with people to brainstorm ways of giving them more agency in how they do their work—and then incorporates those ideas when creating future assignments, development goals, and performance targets. He also examines the pulls that enticed individuals to join his team so that he can deliver—and keep delivering, for as long as possible—on what brought them there. He finds that when he can't offer them more ways to continue growing, it's far better to have an upfront conversation about what's next for them than to delay their inevitable departure. That way employees don't stall in their quests for progress, and his team doesn't stagnate from a loss of energy and productivity.

Develop "Shadow" Job Descriptions

The job application process has become so standardized that most employers don't question it. But it needs a serious rethink—especially if you're trying to create a workplace that employees will want to rehire each day after they've joined the organization.

Perhaps the most fundamental problem to solve is the job description. It usually consists of a hodgepodge of skills, qualifications, and platitudes about work style and culture cribbed from past job descriptions, competitors' postings, and requirements for title and pay grades. The whole thing is so broad as to be meaningless—and it's often impossible (and unnecessary) to fill the role as described. No wonder prospective employees puff up their résumés to make themselves look like superheroes. People on both sides of the process—employers and candidates—know that these posts don't reflect reality.

The origin of the job description dates back more than a century. Observing factories in the industrial economy, Frederick

Taylor (whose scientific management theory changed how work was organized and assessed) set out to measure the precise time it took to do various jobs and tasks. After that it was relatively simple to describe the work and its requirements in job postings. Employers kept these descriptions short because newspapers charged by the line to run them.

When job boards went online and charged one flat fee regardless of length, descriptions swelled. Postings quickly morphed into ridiculous wish lists of capabilities and credentials. Companies' legal departments got involved in writing and approving—and further inflating—the language to give their organizations maximum leeway and protection in talent decisions. Maury Hanigan, the CEO of the job-marketing platform SparcStart, says that job descriptions have become "the basis against which an employee is evaluated and potentially fired." Given that purpose, they work poorly as marketing documents and do little to ensure good matches between people and roles. Hanigan likens using them that way to "selling a house by posting the mortgage documents." But it's how things are done.

The litigiousness around employment decisions in our society means that's unlikely to change anytime soon. So hiring managers must work around these vague, bloated descriptions to find the right people. Thus when you reach out to friends and industry contacts for leads and start interacting with candidates, you'll need to create a "shadow" description that supplements the official one to clarify what the person you hire will actually do in the role. It can be useful to borrow concrete descriptions of activities and tasks from performance reviews of people who are already doing the job effectively.

It also helps to focus on the job's *experiences,* not *features.* To illustrate what we mean by that, let's return to the house-listing analogy. Like most job descriptions, real estate postings tend to focus on features, such as open kitchens, home offices, and finished basements. But those things matter only in the context of day-to-day experience: How will people use them when they cook, when they work at home, and when they entertain? That's what the real estate agent helps them envision during a walk-through. You can take a similar approach when giving a private, informal "tour" of the job you're trying to fill. Briefly describe a "day in the life," and offer to chat so that you can provide more practical details. Without those extra layers of information, people will get lost in a hazy job description—or they'll just keep scrolling for a more obvious fit.

Consider this disguised LinkedIn posting for a chief of staff role:

> *Serve as a key member of leadership team. Play critical role in developing, accelerating, and communicating agenda for executing vision. Be responsible for coordinating and advancing companywide priorities and projects. Duties include leading staff units in C-level office; developing and implementing key initiatives; managing special projects and crisis situations; collaborating with senior officers to advance priorities; involvement in comprehensive communications planning and stakeholder engagement; leading and partnering with key staffers and leaders on special projects, operational decisions, policy development, and communications planning.*

After a few more vague sentences the description moves on to requirements:

> *Bachelor's degree; at least 10 years of experience in publications or communications; excellent writing,*

editing, and project management skills; an appreciation for the distinctive culture and values of the organization; ability to strategize creatively and collaboratively; ability to make complex information comprehensible and compelling for a wide range of readers and to write effectively in many styles depending on audience, content, and platform. Proficiency with Microsoft Office, Drupal, social media platforms, and Adobe Creative Suite; initiative; and judgment and discretion when dealing with complex, confidential, and sensitive information.

Now suppose you're trying to fill that role. Without more specifics about what it entails day-to-day, the requirements lack meaning. For example, what does "excellent writing" mean in this context? What is being written, and for what purposes? Who are these audiences that require "many styles"? People will have no idea if you don't tell them. What's meant by "crisis situations"? How will the chief of staff attend to them? What kinds of "companywide priorities and projects" will this new hire manage? What will that look like in practice?

Filling in such specifics allows people to see themselves in a role. If it's simply not a good fit, they—and you—will recognize that sooner. If both sides are still interested, however, you can delve into how the day-to-day experiences might be tailored to the individual. To a strong candidate for a consulting role, for example, you might say, "Within six months we can get you a travel assignment in a region you want to learn more about." Or "By the time you have a year's experience, you'll own some client relationships—and in the meantime, while you're learning, I'll bring you to half my client meetings."

To prevent misunderstandings or broken promises later, especially given how easily managers can lose sight of informal arrangements in the heat of getting an organization's work done, we suggest summarizing any agreements in written communications with candidates. You can document them more formally post-hire in performance-management goals, mentor- or sponsor-meeting templates, and so forth. By working with employees to incorporate the experiences they value most in their development materials, you can create clearer paths to those experiences and make good on your agreements. That's a more meaningful way to keep people engaged than throwing them random "opportunities"—prizes that can feel good in the moment but may end up distracting them from what they really want at work.

By focusing on what someone will *do* (much as you would in a contract agreement for a gig worker) rather than describing what the person will *be* (in the example above, a chief of staff with a laundry list of skills), you can help job seekers gauge whether a role is compatible with the activities that bring them energy, the skills they want to invest in, and the trade-offs they're willing to make in their lives. That level of specificity will also encourage them to represent themselves more accurately in their résumés and interviews. Both sides will get a clearer sense of fit. The new hire can hit the ground running, and you'll have established shared expectations for development and performance—a foundation that you can build on together.

Huddle with HR

When we present our findings to chief human resources officers, they often wonder how they could persuade managers and employees to devote sufficient time and reflection to following our recommendations. That effort does take time—but probably less than you assume, especially if you and your HR team undertake it systematically, in combination with other HR processes.

First, work together to decide how to introduce employees to this new way of thinking about progress. For instance, during onboarding you might familiarize people with the concepts and how they fit into your organization's talent processes. That will help when you sit down later to conduct interviews about their previous roles.

IDRsolutions, a software company in the United Kingdom, has added these conversations to its regular development and review practices. Employees are encouraged to talk about what motivates them and what might cause them to leave so that their personal goals can be better reflected in their job goals. The CEO, Mark Stephens, told us that this lets workers have concrete conversations about what's blocking their progress and enables managers to "preempt people leaving for the wrong reasons because we failed to diagnose an issue early."

Next, work with each employee and HR to design, modify, or find a role that amounts to real progress on both sides. All too often organizations cobble together roles to fit assumptions about what they "should" entail. Or a manager and HR combine whatever responsibilities they must to convince a compensation expert in the finance department that the resulting role can be "graded" at the title and pay level they want. When you understand the effect of pushes and pulls, you can make roles more malleable to better suit people you value. A straightforward way to do that is to transparently and collaboratively examine the tasks within a set of jobs, identify where they can be divided and reassigned cleanly, and mix and match them to create new roles that play to people's strengths and desires.

Zappos, the online shoe and clothing retailer, provides an extreme example of flexible role design. In 2013 the company moved to Holacracy, a decentralized approach to organizing work, whereby employees make the rules, set goals and targets, and form and disband teams fluidly. On average, Zappos employees went from having one role before the transformation to having 7.4 specialized, modular, and often unrelated roles afterward. For example, the same person could simultaneously serve as a taxonomy architect on one project, a user experience designer on another, and a social media manager on a third. Roles rapidly changed to support new goals and initiatives. Slicing roles more thinly complicated things, such as keeping track of who did what and paying people fairly. But, our research shows, a key benefit was that employees could craft their own jobs within the scope of the organization's strategic needs.

Few companies fully embrace a role-selection system like Holacracy, and some that try to do so end up abandoning it because it's a huge commitment of energy to work *on* the organization while working *within* it. (Even Zappos has diverged from aspects of pure Holacracy. It eliminated the time-consuming system of employee self-governance while retaining the modular approach to roles.) But the more finely you can slice roles and tasks, the more opportunity you'll have to design jobs that find the sweet spot between organizational needs and individual progress.

There are many ways to mix and match people and work. What your organization considers a "side gig" in relation to a particular role could become an employee's main gig—and that's OK, as long as all the work gets done well. People eager to branch out might be encouraged to experiment in other functions or business units with short-term assignments, project work, or even discrete experiences (such as attending a sales kickoff meeting or a strategy offsite) that match their definition of progress. Temporary "role slices" like these can be quite small—veritable slivers that provide exposure to new ideas, people, and ways of working. Or they can be bigger and longer-term, such as lateral moves within an internal job market where talent is deployed and developed across team or unit boundaries. A number of companies have created talent marketplaces to facilitate such internal mobility. (See "How to Design an Internal Talent Marketplace," HBR, May–June 2023.) By making such opportunities possible, an employer can continue to reap returns on its talent investments while supporting employees in their individual quests.

When we shared these observations with a group of highly experienced HR professionals, a few asked politely, albeit critically: "Isn't all this just repackaged 'work on good job design,' which dates back to the 1960s and 1970s?" Perhaps, but with this caveat: Technology has made it far easier today than it was back then to support individual job enrichment. We now have digital tools for collaboration, like Slack and Teams, so we can more easily see how people are faring in their interactions with colleagues and what kinds of roadblocks they encounter in their daily work. We have virtual learning tools. We have access to real-time data and analytics about employee behavior that shed light on engagement, productivity, learning, and even happiness. As career paths become less linear and roles become more disaggregated—into gigs, agile operating systems, and other channels for talent to flow smoothly from one kind of work to another—managers and their organizations will acquire even more tools to engage and develop people through work design, whether their efforts are viewed as job enrichment, job crafting, or simply helping employees make progress. As Cassie Soady, the chief people officer of GrainCorp, an Australian agribusiness, explained to us, an entire generation of people have seen technology deliver customized user experiences—and they expect customized employee experiences as well.

. . .

Our approach to career development works best when it involves both self-reflection and collective analysis. When all the thinking is left to the individual, the insights aren't quite as rich, and the employer doesn't benefit nearly as much from them.

If you're feeling overloaded as a manager—and exhausted by employees who seem to crave constant feedback—our recommendations may sound like a lot of work. In a session with the top 500 leaders of a global financial services firm, one senior executive said she was tired of a generation who expected to be "massaged like Wagyu beef" in order to be retained. Fair enough.

But here's the counterargument: The adage "Work smarter . . . not harder" applies. Too many retention and development efforts are one-offs—taxing for managers and less than fruitful for employees. By embedding quests for progress into your talent processes, you can systematically make more-targeted investments in people. That's progress we all want to make.

Originally published in November–December 2024. Reprint S24061

8

The Feedback Fallacy

by Marcus Buckingham and
Ashley Goodall

The debate about feedback at work isn't new. Since at least the middle of the last century, the question of how to get employees to improve has generated a good deal of opinion and research. But recently the discussion has taken on new intensity. The ongoing experiment in "radical transparency" at Bridgewater Associates and the culture at Netflix, which the *Wall Street Journal* recently described as "encouraging harsh feedback" and subjecting workers to "intense and awkward" real-time 360s, are but two examples of the overriding belief that the way to increase performance in companies is through rigorous, frequent, candid, pervasive, and often critical feedback.

How should we give and receive feedback? we wonder. How much, and how often, and using which new app? And, given the hoopla over the approaches of Bridgewater and Netflix, how hard-edged and fearlessly candid should we be? Behind those questions, however, is another question that we're missing, and it's a crucial one. The search for ways to give and receive better feedback assumes that feedback is always useful. But the only reason we're pursuing it is to help people do better. And when we examine *that*—asking, *How can we help each person thrive and excel?*—we find that the answers take us in a different direction.

To be clear, instruction—telling people what steps to follow or what factual knowledge they're lacking—can be truly useful: That's why we have checklists in airplane cockpits and, more recently, in operating rooms. There is indeed a right way for a nurse to give an injection safely, and if you as a novice nurse miss one of the steps, or if you're unaware of critical facts about a patient's condition, then someone should tell you. But the occasions when the actions or knowledge necessary to minimally perform a job can be objectively defined in advance are rare and becoming rarer. What we mean by "feedback" is very different. Feedback is about telling people what we think of their performance and how they should do it better—whether they're giving an effective presentation, leading a team, or creating a strategy. And on that, the research is clear: Telling people what we think of their performance doesn't help them thrive and excel, and telling people how we think they should improve actually *hinders* learning.

Underpinning the current conviction that feedback is an unalloyed good are three theories that we in the business world commonly accept as truths. The first is that other people are more aware than you are of your weaknesses, and that the best way to help you, therefore, is for them to show you what you cannot see for yourself. We can call this our *theory of the source of truth*. You do not realize that your suit is shabby, that your presentation is boring, or that your voice is grating, so it is up to your colleagues

Idea in Brief

The Challenge

Managers today are bombarded with calls to give feedback—constantly, directly, and critically. But it turns out that telling people what we think of their performance and how they can do better is not the best way to help them excel and, in fact, can hinder development.

The Reality

Research shows that, first, we aren't the reliable raters of other people's performance that we think we are; second, criticism inhibits the brain's ability to learn; and, third, excellence is idiosyncratic, can't be defined in advance, and isn't the opposite of failure. Managers can't "correct" a person's way to excellence.

The Solution

Managers need to help their team members see what's working, stopping them with a "Yes! That!" and sharing their experience of what the person did well.

---

to tell you as plainly as possible "where you stand." If they didn't, you would never know, and this would be bad.

The second belief is that the process of learning is like filling up an empty vessel: You lack certain abilities you need to acquire, so your colleagues should teach them to you. We can call this our *theory of learning*. If you're in sales, how can you possibly close deals if you don't learn the competency of "mirroring and matching" the prospect? If you're a teacher, how can you improve if you don't learn and practice the steps in the latest team-teaching technique or "flipped classroom" format? The thought is that you can't—and that you need feedback to develop the skills you're missing.

And the third belief is that great performance is universal, analyzable, and describable, and that once defined, it can be transferred from one person to another, regardless of who each individual is. Hence you can, with feedback about what excellence looks like, understand where you fall short of this ideal and then strive to remedy your shortcomings. We can call this our *theory of excellence*. If you're a manager, your boss might show you the company's supervisor-behaviors model, hold you up against it, and tell you what you need to do to more closely hew to it. If you aspire to lead, your firm might use a 360-degree feedback tool to measure you against its predefined leadership competencies and then suggest various courses or experiences that will enable you to acquire the competencies that your results indicate you lack.

What these three theories have in common is self-centeredness: They take our own expertise and what we are sure is our colleagues' inexpertise as givens; they assume that my way is necessarily your way. But as it turns out, in extrapolating from what creates our own performance to what might create performance in others, we overreach.

Research reveals that none of these theories is true. The more we depend on them, and the more technology we base on them, the *less* learning and productivity we will get from others. To understand why and to see the path to a more effective way of improving performance, let's look more closely at each theory in turn.

The Source of Truth

The first problem with feedback is that humans are unreliable raters of other humans. Over the past 40 years psychometricians have shown in study after study that people don't have the objectivity to hold in their heads a stable definition of an abstract quality, such as *business acumen* or *assertiveness*, and then accurately evaluate someone else on it. Our evaluations are deeply colored by our own understanding of what we're rating others on, our own sense of what good looks like for a particular competency, our harshness or leniency as raters, and our own inherent and unconscious biases. This phenomenon is called the *idiosyncratic rater effect*, and it's large (more than half of your rating of someone else reflects your characteristics, not hers) and resilient (no training can lessen it). In other words, the research shows that feedback is more distortion than truth.

This is why, despite all the training available on how to *receive* feedback, it's such hard work: Recipients have to struggle through this forest of distortion in search of something that they recognize as themselves.

And because your feedback to others is always more you than them, it leads to systematic error, which is magnified when ratings are considered in aggregate. There are only two sorts of measurement error in the world: *random* error, which you can reduce by averaging many readings; and *systematic* error, which you can't. Unfortunately, we all seem to have left math class remembering the former and not the latter. We've built all our performance and leadership feedback tools as though assessment errors are random, and they're not. They're systematic.

Consider color blindness. If we ask a color-blind person to rate the redness of a particular rose, we won't trust his feedback—we know that he is incapable of seeing, let alone "rating," red. His error isn't random; it's predictable and explainable, and it stems from a flaw in his measurement system; hence, it's systematic. If we then decide to ask seven more color-blind people to rate the redness of our rose, their errors will be equally systematic, and averaging their ratings won't get us any closer to determining the actual redness of the rose. In fact, it's worse than this.

Adding up all the inaccurate redness ratings—"gray," "pretty gray," "whitish gray," "muddy brown," and so on—and averaging them leads us *further away* both from learning anything reliable about the individuals' personal experiences of the rose and from the actual truth of how red our rose really is.

What the research has revealed is that we're all color-blind when it comes to abstract attributes, such as *strategic thinking, potential,* and *political savvy*. Our inability to rate others on them is predictable and explainable—it is systematic. We cannot remove the error by adding more data inputs and averaging them out, and doing that actually makes the error bigger.

Worse still, although science has long since proven that we are color-blind, in the business world we assume we're clear-eyed. Deep down we don't think we make very many errors at all. We think we're reliable raters of others. We think we're a source of truth. We aren't. We're a source of error.

When a feedback instrument surveys eight colleagues about your business acumen, your score of 3.79 is far greater a distortion than if it simply surveyed one person about you—the 3.79 number is *all* noise, no signal. Given that (a) we're starting to see more of this sort of data-based feedback, (b) this data on you will likely be kept by your company for a very long time, and (c) it will be used to pay, promote, train, and deploy or fire you, you should be worried about just how fundamentally flawed it really is.

The only realm in which humans are an unimpeachable source of truth is that of their own feelings and experiences. Doctors have long known this. When they check up on you post-op, they'll ask, "On a scale of one to 10, with 10 being high, how would you rate your pain?" And if you say, "Five," the doctor may then prescribe all manner of treatments, but what she's unlikely to do is challenge you on your "five." It doesn't make sense, no matter how many operations she has done, to tell you your "five" is wrong, and that, actually, this morning your pain is a "three." It doesn't make sense to try to parse what you mean by "five," and whether any cultural differences might indicate that your "five" is not, in fact, a real "five." It doesn't make sense to hold calibration sessions with other doctors to ensure that your "five" is the same as the other "fives" in the rooms down the hall. Instead, she can be confident that you are the best judge of your pain and that all she can know for sure is that you will be feeling better when you rate your pain lower. Your rating is yours, not hers.

Just as your doctor doesn't know the truth of your pain, we don't know the truth about our colleagues, at least not in any objective way. You may read that workers today—especially Millennials—want to know where they stand. You may occasionally have team members ask you to tell them where they stand, objectively. You may feel that it's your duty to try to answer these questions. But you can't—none of us can. All we can do—and it's not nothing—is share our own feelings and experiences, our own reactions. Thus we can tell someone whether his voice grates *on us;* whether he's persuasive *to us;* whether his presentation is boring *to us.* We may not be able to tell him where he stands, but we can tell him where he stands *with us.* Those are our truths, not his. This is a humbler claim, but at least it's accurate.

How We Learn

Another of our collective theories is that feedback contains useful information, and that this information is the magic ingredient that will accelerate someone's learning. Again, the research points in the opposite direction. Learning is less a function of adding something that isn't there than it is of recognizing, reinforcing, and refining what already is. There are two reasons for this.

The first is that, neurologically, we grow more in our areas of greater ability (our strengths are our development areas). The brain continues to develop throughout life, but each person's does so differently. Because of your genetic inheritance and the oddities of your early childhood environment, your brain's wiring is utterly unique. Some parts of it have tight thickets of synaptic connections, while others are far less dense, and these patterns are different from one person to the next. According to brain science, people grow far more neurons and synaptic connections where they already have the most neurons and synaptic connections. In other words, each brain grows most where it's already strongest. As Joseph LeDoux, a professor of neuroscience at New York University, memorably described it, "Added connections are therefore more like new buds on a branch rather than new branches." Through this lens, learning looks a lot like building, little by little, on the unique patterns already there within you. Which in turn means learning has to start by finding and understanding those patterns—your patterns, not someone else's.

Second, getting attention to our strengths from others catalyzes learning, whereas attention to our weaknesses smothers it. Neurological science also shows what happens to us when other people focus on what's working within us instead of remediating what isn't. In one experiment scientists split students into two groups. To one group they gave positive coaching, asking the students about their dreams and how they'd go about achieving them. The scientists probed the other group about homework and what the students thought they were doing wrong and needed to fix. While those conversations were happening, the scientists hooked each student up to a functional magnetic resonance imaging machine to see which parts of the brain were most activated in response to these different sorts of attention.

In the brains of the students asked about what they needed to correct, the sympathetic nervous system lit up. This is the "fight or flight" system, which mutes the other parts of the brain and allows us to focus only on the information most necessary to survive. Your brain responds to critical feedback as a threat and narrows its activity. The strong negative emotion produced by criticism "inhibits access to existing neural circuits and invokes cognitive, emotional, and perceptual impairment," psychology and business professor Richard Boyatzis said in summarizing the researchers' findings.

Focusing people on their shortcomings or gaps doesn't enable learning. It impairs it.

In the students who focused on their dreams and how they might achieve them, the sympathetic nervous system was not activated. What lit up instead was the parasympathetic nervous system, sometimes referred to as the "rest and digest" system. To quote Boyatzis again: "The parasympathetic nervous system . . . stimulates adult neurogenesis (i.e., growth of new neurons) . . . , a sense of well-being, better immune system functioning, and cognitive, emotional, and perceptual openness."

What findings such as these show us is, first, that learning happens when we see how we might do something better by adding some new nuance or expansion to our own understanding. Learning rests on our grasp of what we're doing well, not on what we're doing poorly, and certainly not on someone else's sense of what we're doing poorly. And second, that we learn most when someone else pays attention to what's working within us and asks us to cultivate it intelligently. We're often told that the key to learning is to get out of our comfort zones, but these findings contradict that particular chestnut: Take us very far out of our comfort zones, and our brains stop paying attention to anything other than surviving the experience. It's clear that we learn most in our comfort zones, because that's where our neural pathways are most concentrated. It's where we're most open to possibility, most creative, insightful, and productive. That's where feedback must meet us—in our moments of flow.

Excellence

We spend the bulk of our working lives pursuing excellence in the belief that while defining it is easy, the really hard part is codifying how we and everyone else on our team should get there. We've got it backward: Excellence in any endeavor is almost impossible to define, and yet getting there, for each of us, is relatively easy.

Excellence is idiosyncratic. Take funniness—the ability to make others laugh. If you watch early Steve Martin clips, you might land on the idea that excellence at it means strumming a banjo, waggling your knees, and wailing, "I'm a wild and crazy guy!" But watch Jerry Seinfeld, and you might conclude that it means talking about nothing in a slightly annoyed, exasperated tone. And if you watch Sarah Silverman, you might think to yourself, no, it's being caustic, blunt, and rude in an incongruously affectless way. At this point you may begin to perceive the truth that "funny" is inherent to the person.

Watch an NBA game, and you may think to yourself, "Yes, most of them are tall and athletic, but boy, not only does each player have a different role on the team, but even the players in the same role on the same team seem to do it differently." Examine something as specific and as limited as the free throws awarded after fouls, and you'll learn that not only do the top two free-throw shooters in history have utterly different styles, but one of them, Rick Barry—the best ever on the day he retired (look him up)—didn't even throw overhand.

Excellence seems to be inextricably and wonderfully intertwined with whoever demonstrates it. Each person's version of it is uniquely shaped and is an expression of that person's individuality. Which means that, for each of us, excellence is easy, in that it is a natural, fluid, and intelligent expression of our best extremes. It can be cultivated, but it's unforced.

Excellence is also not the opposite of failure. But in virtually all aspects of human endeavor, people assume that it is and that if they study what leads to pathological functioning and do the reverse—or replace what they found missing—they can create optimal functioning. That assumption is flawed. Study disease and you will learn a lot about disease and precious little about health. Eradicating depression will get you no closer to joy. Divorce is mute on the topic of happy marriage. Exit interviews with employees who leave tell you nothing about why others stay. If you study failure, you'll learn a lot about failure but nothing about how to achieve excellence. Excellence has its own pattern.

And it's even more problematic than that. Excellence and failure often have a lot in common. So if you study ineffective leaders and observe that they have big egos, and then argue that good leaders should not have big egos, you will lead people astray. Why? Because when you do personality assessments with highly effective leaders, you discover that they have very strong egos as well. Telling someone that you must lose your ego to be a good leader is flawed advice. Likewise, if you study poor salespeople, discover that they take rejection personally, and then tell a budding salesperson to avoid doing the same, your advice will be misguided. Why? Because rigorous studies of the best salespeople reveal that they take rejection deeply personally, too.

As it happens, you find that effective leaders put their egos in the service of others, not themselves, and that effective salespeople take rejection personally because they are personally invested in the sale—but the point is that you will never find these things out by studying *ineffective* performance.

Since excellence is idiosyncratic and cannot be learned by studying failure, we can never help another person succeed by holding her performance up against a prefabricated model of excellence, giving her feedback on where she misses the model, and telling her to plug the gaps. That approach will only ever get her to adequate performance. Point out the grammatical flaws in an essay, ask the writer to fix the flaws, and while you may get an essay with good grammar, you won't get a piece of writing that transports the reader. Show a new teacher when her students lost interest and tell her what to do to fix this, and while you may now have a teacher whose students don't fall asleep in class, you won't have one whose students necessarily learn any more.

How to Help People Excel

If we continue to spend our time identifying failure as we see it and giving people feedback about how to avoid it, we'll languish in the business of adequacy. To get into the excellence business we need some new techniques:

Look for outcomes. Excellence is an outcome, so take note of when a prospect leans into a sales pitch, a project runs smoothly, or an angry customer suddenly calms down. Then turn to the team member who created the outcome and say, "That! Yes, that!" By doing this, you'll stop the flow of work for a moment and pull your colleague's attention back toward something she just did that really worked.

There's a story about how legendary Dallas Cowboys coach Tom Landry turned around his struggling team. While the other teams were reviewing missed tackles and dropped balls, Landry instead combed through footage of previous games and created for each player a highlight reel of when he had done something easily, naturally, and effectively. Landry reasoned that while the number of wrong ways to do something was infinite, the number of right ways, for any particular player, was not. It was knowable, and the best way to discover it was to look at plays where that person had done it excellently. From now on, he told each team member, "we only replay your winning plays."

Now on one level he was doing this to make his team members feel better about themselves because he knew the power of praise. But according to the story, Landry wasn't nearly as interested in praise as he was in learning. His instincts told him that each person would improve his performance most if he could see, in slow motion, what his own personal version of excellence looked like.

You can do the same. Whenever you see one of your people do something that worked for you, that rocked your world just a little, stop for a minute and highlight it. By helping your team member recognize what excellence looks like for her—by saying, "That! Yes, that!"—you're offering her the chance to gain an insight; you're highlighting a pattern that is already there within her so that she can recognize it, anchor it, re-create it, and refine it. That is learning.

Replay your instinctive reactions. Unlike Landry, you're not going to be able to videotape your people. Instead, learn how to replay to them your own personal reactions. The key is not to tell someone how well she's performed or how good she is. While simple praise isn't a bad thing, you are by no means the authority on what objectively good performance is, and instinctively she knows this. Instead, describe what you experienced when her moment of excellence caught your attention. There's nothing more believable and more authoritative than sharing what you saw from her and how it made you feel. Use phrases such as "This is how that came across for me," or "This is what that made me think," or even just "Did you see what you did there?" Those are your reactions—they are your truth—and when you relay them in specific detail, you aren't judging or rating or fixing her; you're simply reflecting to her the unique "dent" she just made in the world, as seen through your eyes. And precisely because it isn't a judgment or a rating it is at once more humble and more powerful.

On the flip side, if you're the team member, whenever your team leader catches you doing something right, ask her to pause and describe her reaction to you. If she says, "Good job!" ask, "Which bit? What did you see that seemed to work well?" Again, the point of this isn't to pile on the praise. The point is to explore the nature of excellence, and this is surely a better object for all the energy currently being pointed at "radical transparency" and the like. We're so close to our own performance that it's hard to get perspective on it and see its patterns and components. Ask for your leader's help in rendering the unconscious, conscious—so that you can understand it, improve at it, and, most important, do it again.

The Right Way to Help Colleagues Excel

If you want to get into the excellence business, here are some examples of language to try.

Instead of	Try
Can I give you some feedback?	Here's my reaction.
Good job!	Here are three things that really worked for me. What was going through your mind when you did them?
Here's what you should do.	Here's what I would do.
Here's where you need to improve.	Here's what worked best for me, and here's why.
That didn't really work.	When you did x, I felt y or I didn't get that.
You need to improve your communication skills.	Here's exactly where you started to lose me.
You need to be more responsive.	When I don't hear from you, I worry that we're not on the same page.
You lack strategic thinking.	I'm struggling to understand your plan.
You should do x [in response to a request for advice].	What do you feel you're struggling with, and what have you done in the past that's worked in a similar situation?

Never lose sight of your highest-priority interrupt. In computing a high-priority interrupt happens when something requires a computer processor's immediate attention, and the machine halts normal operations and jumps the urgent issue to the head of the processing queue. Like computer processors, team leaders have quite a few things that demand their attention and force them to act. Many of them are problems. If you see something go off the rails—a poorly handled call, a missed meeting, a project gone awry—the instinct will kick in to stop everything to tell someone what she did wrong and what she needs to do to fix it. This instinct is by no means misguided: If your team member screws something up, you have to deal with it. But remember that when you do, you're merely remediating—and that remediating not only inhibits learning but also gets you no closer to excellent performance. As we've seen, conjuring excellence from your team members requires a different focus from you. If you see somebody doing something that really works, stopping her and dissecting it with her isn't only a high-priority interrupt, it is your *highest*-priority interrupt. As you replay each small moment of excellence to your team member, you'll ease her into the "rest and digest" state of mind. Her understanding of what excellence looks and feels like within her will become more vivid, her brain will become more receptive to new information and will make connections to other inputs found in other regions of her brain, and she will learn and grow and get better.

Explore the present, past, and future. When people come to you asking for feedback on their performance or what they might need to fix to get promoted, try this:

Start with the *present*. If a team member approaches you with a problem, he's dealing with it *now*. He's feeling weak or challenged, and you have to address that. But rather than tackling the problem head-on, ask your colleague to tell you three things that are working for him *right now*. These things might be related to the situation or entirely separate. They might be significant or trivial. Just ask the question, and you're priming him with oxytocin—which is sometimes called the "love drug" but which here is better thought of as the "creativity drug." Getting him to think about specific things that are going well will alter his brain chemistry so that he can be open to new solutions and new ways of thinking or acting.

Next, go to the *past*. Ask him, "When you had a problem like this in the past, what did you do that worked?" Much of our life happens in patterns, so it's highly likely that he has encountered this problem at least a few times before. On one of those occasions he will almost certainly have found some way forward, some action or insight or connection that enabled him to move out of the mess. Get him thinking about that and seeing it in his mind's eye: what he actually felt and did, and what happened next.

Finally, turn to the *future*. Ask your team member, "What do you already know you need to do? What do you already know works in this situation?" By all means offer up one or two of your own experiences to see if they might clarify his own. But operate under the assumption that he already knows the solution—you're just helping him recognize it.

The emphasis here should not be on whys—"Why didn't that work?" "Why do you think you should do that?"—because those lead both of you into a fuzzy world of conjecture and concepts. Instead, focus on the whats—"What do you actually want to have happen?" "What are a couple of actions you could take right now?" These sorts of questions yield concrete answers, in which your colleague can find his actual self doing actual things in the near-term future.

. . .

How to give people feedback is one of the hottest topics in business today. The arguments for radical candor and unvarnished and pervasive transparency have a swagger to them, almost as if to imply that only the finest and bravest of us can face these truths with nerveless self-assurance, that those of us who recoil at the thought of working in a climate of continual judgment are condemned to mediocrity, and that as leaders our ability to look our colleagues squarely in the eye and lay out their faults without blinking is a measure of our integrity.

But at best, this fetish with feedback is good only for correcting mistakes—in the rare cases where the right steps are known and can be evaluated objectively. And at worst, it's toxic, because what we want from our people—and from ourselves—is not, for the most part, tidy adherence to a procedure agreed upon in advance or, for that matter, the ability to expose one another's flaws. It's that people contribute their own unique and growing talents to a common good, when that good is ever-evolving, when we are, for all the right reasons, making it up as we go along. Feedback has nothing to offer to that.

We humans do not do well when someone whose intentions are unclear tells us where we stand, how good we "really" are, and what we must do to fix ourselves. We excel *only* when people who know us and care about us tell us what they experience and what they feel, and in particular when they see something within us that really works.

Originally published in March–April 2019. Reprint R1902G

QUICK READ

To Excel, Diverse Teams Need Psychological Safety

by Henrik Bresman and Amy C. Edmondson

When teaching groups of executives, we often ask them how diversity affects teams' performance. The vast majority are convinced that more-diverse teams will outperform less-diverse teams—particularly when the project involves innovation. Their argument is familiar: The different perspectives, ideas, and opinions in diverse teams are essential to achieving breakthrough performance in competitive environments.

In practice, however, diverse teams often underperform relative to homogenous teams. Why? They face communication challenges that get in the way of their undeniable potential. It's simple. People with similar backgrounds share norms and assumptions about how to behave, how to set priorities, and at what pace to do the work. When team members come from different backgrounds, these taken-for-granted habits frequently clash.[1] Even what counts as evidence to support an opinion varies across fields. The result is misunderstanding and frustration. Indeed, past research suggests that, on average, demographic diversity has a negative effect on teams' outcomes.[2]

Our research in drug development, an innovation-intensive setting, suggests that team psychological safety—a shared belief that team members will not be rejected or embarrassed for speaking up with their ideas, questions, or concerns—may hold the key to unlocking the benefits of diversity.[3]

Initial Evidence

The theory that psychological safety may be the key to realizing the promise of diversity in teams is not new.[4] But empirical evidence that it's true has been lacking. So we set out to test this idea empirically in a study of 62 drug development teams at six large pharmaceutical firms whose makeup had varying degrees of diversity. The diverse teams' work involved collaborating with external partners, meeting tight deadlines, and developing drugs that had to meet high regulatory standards for safety and efficacy. We measured diversity using a composite index (including gender, age, tenure, and functional expertise) and psychological safety using an established survey measure. We collected team performance ratings from senior leaders in the companies, who were unaware of the teams' values on our other measures.

Here is what we found. As predicted, on average, team diversity had a slight negative effect on performance. However, in those teams with high psychological safety, diversity was positively associated with performance. By contrast, diversity was even more negatively associated with performance for teams with lower psychological safety than the average. Although ours

Idea in Brief

The Problem
Despite the common perception that more diverse teams outperform less diverse teams when it comes to achieving breakthrough performance, communication challenges often get in the way of diverse teams' potential.

The Context
People with similar backgrounds tend to share norms and assumptions about how to behave, set priorities, and pace work that reduce friction. When team members come from different backgrounds, however, alignment around such habits and beliefs can result in misunderstandings and frustration that impede group performance.

The Solution
Research shows that building psychological safety—a shared belief that team members won't be rejected or embarrassed for speaking up—may hold the key to unlocking the benefits of diversity on teams.

---

is only a single study in a single industry and more research is required to confirm our findings, our data supports the compelling arguments about the role of psychological safety in unlocking the potential of diverse teams.

Another finding—one that's especially important in times of high turnover—is that team diversity was inversely correlated with members' satisfaction with their team: On average, people were less happy with their team the more diverse it was. But for the subset of teams with high levels of psychological safety, the more diverse the teams, the more satisfied their members were. In short, psychological safety appears to help teams realize the potential of diversity for both performance and well-being.

We recommend three ways for diverse teams to build psychologically safe environments, starting with team leaders: framing, inquiry, and bridging boundaries.

Psychological safety, diversity, and team performance

In a study of 62 drug development teams at six large pharmaceutical firms whose makeup had varying degrees of diversity, those that were diverse and psychologically safe outperformed comparably diverse teams that lacked psychological safety.

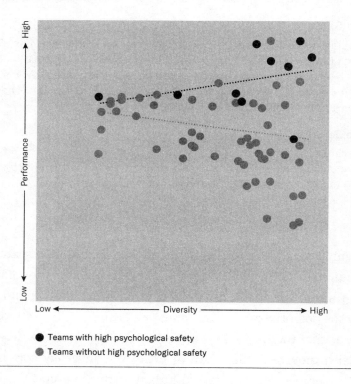

● Teams with high psychological safety
● Teams without high psychological safety

Framing

Framing is about helping team members reach a common understanding of the work and the context. Two frames are particularly relevant for diverse teams: goals for the meeting and the value of expertise.

Frame meetings as opportunities for information-sharing. Most team meetings are implicitly framed as updating and decision-making encounters—a framing associated with judgment and evaluation. This frame makes people less willing to speak up and raise questions or concerns and offer novel ideas. To override this default frame, it helps to open a meeting by making the sharing of information and ideas an explicit goal. Then, make sure to systematically invite people with different perspectives to join the conversation, one by one, and listen to and capture what they have to say before moving on to consider the implications of these perspectives and make decisions.

Frame differences as a source of value. All of us are prone to being frustrated by differences in opinion or perspective. Even if we recognize differences as sources of potential value and opportunities for learning, overcoming our instinctive preference for agreement takes effort. Being explicit in framing differences as a source of value can help. For instance, say: "We are likely to have different perspectives going into this meeting, which will help us arrive at a fuller understanding of the issues in this decision (or project)."

Inquiry

The best way to help people contribute their thoughts is to ask them to do so. It's that simple. When team leaders—and others—practice genuine inquiry that draws out others' ideas, listening thoughtfully to what they hear in response, psychological safety in the team grows. The need for inquiry is heightened in diverse teams because of the number and variety of perspectives represented. But inquiry is rarely spontaneous; all of us bring blind spots to our teams—gaps in knowledge or understanding of which we are unaware—and we virtually never ask questions about things we don't know we don't know.

The willingness to listen—really listen—to what others are saying is not a given, particularly in diverse teams. It takes practice and involves asking the right kinds of questions:

Open questions. The most effective questions for leveraging diverse perspectives and experiences lack a predetermined answer and are motivated by a desire to learn. Examples: What do you see in your community? Or, What are you hearing from customers?

Questions that build shared ownership and causality. Questions that reflect the complexity of integrating diverse views comprise a powerful tool. For example: What did I do to put you in a challenging position? How can I help? Contrast this systemic framing with questions that fail to recognize the possibility that you also contributed to the problems or challenges at hand: What did you do to create this situation? What will you do about it?

Bridging Boundaries

Framing and inquiry help build psychologically safe environments. But getting even more tactical, what can individual team members do to bridge expertise and background boundaries? What do they really need to know about each other to gain traction in their collaborative work? They don't have to know each other's entire life story or body of expertise. But they do need to figure out where their objectives, expertise, and challenges come together. Any two people—or members of the entire team—can do that by seeking the following information about each other.

- *Hopes and goals.* What do you want to accomplish?
- *Resources and skills.* What do you bring to the table?
- *Concerns and obstacles.* What are you up against? What are you worried about?

We have found these questions to be surprisingly efficient in providing a foundation for moving forward. They are all task-relevant; none is overly personal, but each requires you to open up and leave yourself vulnerable to others.

While diversity of backgrounds is generally a requirement for breakthrough performance, particularly when seeking innovation, it is rarely sufficient. Diverse teams need the lubricant of psychological safety to ensure that their members ask questions and share ideas. Leaders, and other team members, play a crucial role in nurturing psychological safety through framing, inquiry skills, and a capacity to step in to bridge different perspectives. When this happens, teams stand to gain more than just performance benefits. Effective leadership of diverse teams also builds a healthier work environment and a more satisfying team experience.

Adapted from "Research: To Excel, Diverse Teams Need Psychological Safety" on hbr.org, March 17, 2022. Reprint H06VV8

Managers Can't Do It All

by Diane Gherson and Lynda Gratton

Jennifer stares at her upward-feedback report and wonders how she got to this point. How could a veteran like her, someone who was once celebrated as manager of the year, receive such negative ratings? She used to enjoy her role, but now everything feels out of control. Her job has been reshaped so constantly—by sweeping process reengineering, digitization, and agile initiatives, and most recently by remote work—that she always feels at least one step behind.

The amount of change that has taken place in just the past few years is overwhelming. The management layer above her was eliminated, which doubled the size of her team, and almost half the people on it are now working on cross-division projects led by *other* managers. She and her team used to meet in her office for progress reviews, but now she has no office, and if she wants to know how her people are doing, she has to join their stand-ups, which makes her feel like an onlooker rather than their boss. She no longer feels in touch with how everybody is doing, and yet she has the same set of personnel responsibilities as before: providing performance feedback, making salary adjustments, hiring and firing, engaging in career discussions.

Not only that, but she's being asked to take on even more. Because her company is rapidly digitizing, for example, she's responsible for upgrading her staff's technical skills. This makes her uncomfortable because it feels threatening to many of her team members. When she talks with them about it, she's expected to demonstrate endless amounts of empathy—something that has never been her strong suit. She's supposed to seek out diverse talent and create a climate of psychological safety while simultaneously downsizing the unit. She understands why all these things are important, but they're not what she signed up for when she became a manager, and she's just not sure that she has the emotional energy to handle them.

What happened to the stable, well-defined job that she was so good at for so long? What happened to the power and status that used to come with that job? Is *she* the problem? Is she simply no longer able to keep up with the demands of the evolving workplace? Is she now part of the "frozen middle"—the much-maligned layer of management that obstructs change rather than enables it?

Jennifer—a composite of several real people we have met in our work—has no answers to these questions. All she knows is that she's frustrated, unhappy, and overwhelmed.

As are managers everywhere.

One of us, Lynda, is an academic researcher and consultant to corporations, and the other, Diane, was until her recent retirement the chief human resources officer at IBM (in which she still owns stock). In those roles we have closely observed the changing job of the manager, and we can report that a crisis is looming.

Idea in Brief

The Problem
Managers are the lifeblood of organizations. In recent decades, as the workplace has changed, they've been asked to take on new responsibilities and demonstrate new skills—and are struggling to cope. This threatens productivity, employee well-being, and brand reputation.

The New Reality
Change has come along three dimensions: power (managers have to think about making teams successful, not being served by them); skills (they're expected to coach performance, not oversee tasks); and structure (they have to lead in more-fluid environments).

The Way Forward
We need to do everything we can to help managers adapt. The three companies featured in this article have deliberately—and successfully—transformed the role of manager so that it better meets the demands of 21st-century work.

The signs are everywhere. In 2021, when we asked executives from 60 companies around the world how their managers were doing, we got unanimous reports of frustration and exhaustion. Similarly, when the research firm Gartner asked 75 HR leaders from companies worldwide how their managers were faring, 68% reported that they were overwhelmed. Nonetheless, according to Gartner, only 14% of those companies had taken steps to help alleviate their managers' burdens.

The problem isn't hard to diagnose. The traditional role of the manager evolved in the hierarchical workplaces of the industrial age, but in our fluid, flatter, postindustrial age that role is beginning to look archaic.

The irony is that we actually need great people leaders more than ever. Microsoft has found, for example, that when managers help teams prioritize, nurture their culture, and support work/life balance, employees feel more connected and are more positive about their work. The consulting firm O.C. Tanner has likewise found that weekly one-to-ones with managers during uncertain times lead to a 54% increase in engagement, a 31% increase in productivity, a 15% decrease in burnout, and a 16% decrease in depression among employees. Meanwhile, according to McKinsey, having good relationships with their managers is the top factor in employees' job satisfaction, which in turn is the second-most-important determinant of their overall well-being.

Conversely, bad managers can significantly hurt retention and engagement: Seventy-five percent of the participants in the McKinsey survey reported that the most stressful aspect of their jobs was their immediate boss. As the saying goes, people join companies and leave their managers.

Something is clearly broken. If managers remain essential but their traditional role has become obsolete, then it's obviously time for a change.

In this article we'll make the case for redefining and even splitting the role rather than simply continuing to let it evolve, which is a potentially costly and disastrous course of action. But first let's briefly take stock of the waves of innovation that have brought us to this crisis point.

Four Defining Business Movements

The first wave, *process reengineering*, began about 1990 and lasted until the early 2000s. It focused on eliminating bureaucracy and boosting operational efficiencies. With the help of consulting firms, which developed practices around this kind of work, companies globalized and outsourced their processes, flattened their hierarchies, and in many cases put their remaining managers in "player-coach" roles that required them to take on workers' tasks. These changes reduced costs, but they also made life a lot harder for managers. They now had wider responsibilities and significantly larger teams to supervise and were also expected to dedicate themselves personally to projects and customers.

The next wave of innovation, *digitization,* arrived in about 2010. Promisingly, it democratized access to both information and people, but in doing so it undermined traditional sources of managerial power. CEOs and other senior leaders could now communicate directly with their entire workforces, sharing strategies, priorities, and important updates and responding to concerns. No longer a necessary part of the information loop, managers began to feel a loss of power, control, and status.

Then came the *agile movement* and its process changes, which companies began to adopt in the mid to late 2010s. It aimed to shorten timelines and turbocharge innovation by using internal marketplaces across whole organizations to match skills to work and to rapidly assemble project teams on an as-needed basis. As a result, managers started to lose touch with their reports, who now spent much of their time under the rotating supervision of the project managers they were temporarily assigned to. And because candidates could be matched to openings online, managers lost the power and authority involved with brokering career opportunities for their people.

Finally, a fourth wave arrived in 2020 with the pandemic, when companies and employees were forced to embrace the possibilities of *flexible work*. This was a watershed moment. It dramatically

From manager to people leader

Three fundamental shifts in the role of managers today.

A power shift: from "me" to "we"

My team makes me successful.	→	I'm here to make my team successful.
I'm rewarded for achieving business goals.	→	I'm also rewarded for improving team engagement, inclusion, and skills relevancy.
I control how people move beyond my unit.	→	I scout for talent and help my team move fluidly to wider opportunities.

A skills shift: from task overseer to performance coach

I oversee work.	→	I track outcomes.
I assess team members against expectations.	→	I coach them to achieve their potential and invite their feedback on my management.
I provide work direction and share information from above.	→	I supply inspiration, sensemaking, and emotional support.

A structural shift: from static and physical to fluid and digital

I manage an intact team of people in fixed jobs in a physical workplace.	→	My team is fluid, and the workplace is digital.
I set goals and make assessments annually.	→	I provide ongoing guidance on priorities and performance feedback.
I hold an annual career discussion focused on the next promotion.	→	I'm always retraining my team and providing career coaching.

altered how and where work was done. Once employees were no longer tied to a physical workplace, managers lost the close control that they used to have over employees' performance and behavior—and employees began to realize that they could tap a greater range of job options, far beyond commuting distance from their homes. These changes were liberating, but they placed even more of a burden on managers—who now were also expected to cultivate empathetic relationships that would allow them to engage and retain the people they supervised.

These waves of innovation have changed the role of the manager along three dimensions: *power, skills,* and *structure.* In a power shift, managers have to think about making teams successful, not being served by them. In a skills shift, they're expected to coach performance, not oversee tasks; and in a structural shift, they have to lead in more-fluid environments.

These changes have empowered employees, which of course is a good thing. But they've also altered how managers drive productivity. Organizations are starting to recognize this. When we asked the executives in our 60-company survey to list the most important areas that managers need to focus on today, their top answers were coaching, communication, and employee well-being.

New Models of Management

Some organizations have taken deliberate steps to reimagine the role of the manager. Let's take a look at transformative shifts that have been made at three very different companies in banking, tech, and telecommunications.

Building new skills at scale. Most companies think of their top leaders as the people who make change happen—and are willing to spend millions on their development as a result. The layers of management below the top, the theory goes, are frozen in place and will resist change. But the executives at Standard Chartered—a retail bank, headquartered in London, with more than 750 branches in 50-plus countries—recently chose to think differently. Their 14,000 middle managers, they decided, would play a central role in the bank's growth.

Rather than wholly redesigning the job, the executive team began with some basic steps: changing the role's title, creating an accreditation process, and strengthening the sense of a managerial community. Managers became "people leaders," an acknowledgment of how important the human connection was in their work. Meanwhile, the new accreditation process evaluated future-focused capabilities such as driving growth, building trust, aligning teams, and making bold decisions. And the executive team worked to strengthen community by applying the local experiences of people leaders to problems across the whole company. For example, when in the course of filling 10 positions, one cohort of people leaders failed to hire anybody from an underrepresented group, the executive team didn't single the group out for criticism but instead seized the opportunity to ask the whole community, "How can we support you in making your teams more diverse?"

Next the executive team decided to focus on coaching, which has today become a crucial management skill. (See chapter 3.) Coaching, in fact, plays a key role in each of the three shifts we described earlier: When managers coach they're making a power shift by moving from instruction to support and guidance; a skills shift by moving from the oversight of work to the continual giving of feedback; and a structural shift by engaging with their people in a way that's dynamic and constant rather than static and episodic.

Standard Chartered had been working for decades on developing its top leaders into coaches. But now the challenge was scaling that effort up to 14,000 people leaders. The bank did this through a variety of initiatives—by using an AI-based coaching platform, for example, and by developing peer-to-peer and team coaching across all its markets in Africa, the Middle East, and Asia. It also launched a pilot project in which it offered to help people leaders pay for formal training and accreditation as coaches (by outside organizations approved by the global governing body for coaching). Those who accepted were expected to coach other employees; the goal was building what Tanuj Kapilashrami, the bank's head of human resources, describes as "a deep coaching culture." So many participants reported a boost in skills and confidence that the bank organized further rounds of training and accreditation, each of which was oversubscribed, with hundreds of people taking part around the world.

Rewiring processes and systems. In 2013, as IBM's new chief human resources officer, Diane realized that to support the massive transformation that had been launched by then-CEO Ginni Rometty, the company needed a different kind of manager. IBM was changing 50% of its product portfolio over the next five years, moving into several growth businesses (among them the cloud, AI, cybersecurity, and blockchain), and migrating from software licensing to software as a service. At a worldwide town hall, Rometty announced that all employees would be required not only to develop new skills but also to learn to work differently. The company would build a culture optimized for innovation and speed—and needed its managers to lead retraining efforts, adapt their management styles to agile work methods, and get all employees engaged in the journey.

That meant doing three things: freeing managers up for additional responsibilities by digitally transforming their work; equipping them with new skills; and holding them accountable through a metrics-driven performance-development system. Their most important goal was employee engagement: Managers account for 70% of the variance in that metric.

The HR function deployed AI to eliminate administrative work, such as approving expense reports or transferring employees to a new unit. Personalized digital learning was introduced so that managers could access support on their mobile phones—for, say, just-in-time guidance on preparing for difficult conversations. New AI-driven programs also helped managers make better people decisions and spot issues like attrition risk. An AI-driven adviser has made it easier for managers to determine salary increases: It considers not only performance and market pay gaps but also internal data on employee turnover by skills, the current external demand for each employee's skills (scraped from competitor job postings), and the future demand.

Now when managers have salary conversations with employees, they can confidently share the rationale for their decisions, help team members understand the demand for their skills, and, most important, focus on supporting them as they build market-relevant capabilities and accelerate their career growth.

Like Standard Chartered, IBM also introduced an accreditation for managers, built on a new training curriculum. The impact has been significant: Managers who have obtained this accreditation are scoring five points higher today on employee engagement than those who have not.

In addition, IBM requires managers to get "licenses" in key activities by undergoing an in-house certification program. Licenses to hire, for example, are designed to ensure that managers select candidates in an objective and unbiased way, provide them with a well-designed experience, and ultimately make hires of high quality. The impact has been significant here too: Employees hired by licensed managers are 7% more likely to exceed expectations at six months and 45% less likely to leave the company within their first year than other hires are. Those numbers mean a lot in a company that makes more than 50,000 hires a year.

One major shift is the deliberate change from performance management to performance development. Not just about business results, the new system reflects the mindset and skills needed to manage in the modern workplace.

Feedback is at its core. Team members are asked whether their managers create an environment that encourages candid communication. Do they provide frequent and meaningful feedback? Do they help in the development of market-relevant skills? Are they effective career coaches? At the same time, HR gathers metrics on diversity and inclusion, regretted attrition, and skills development. The company then combines those metrics with its survey data and feeds the results into its Manager Success Index—a dashboard that allows managers to understand how well they're meeting expectations and to identify needs for both learning and "unlearning." Managers are invited to training programs on the basis of their specific development needs. Investing in these programs pays off: People who have completed at least one course in the past two years are 20% less likely to be in the bottom decile of the Manager Success Index, whereas those who have taken no leadership development courses are much more likely to be there.

IBM takes this idea seriously. Managers who do not demonstrate growth behaviors and who consistently underperform get moved out of managerial positions. The message to the company's managers is clear: Times have changed, and you must too. Your ongoing service as a manager is tightly connected to the continued growth and engagement of your people. We're here to support you in rethinking traditional practices, attitudes, and habits, and adopting ones better suited to new ways of working and the digital workplace.

Splitting the role of the manager. Telstra, a $16 billion Australian telecommunications company that employs more than 32,000 people, has made perhaps the boldest move. When Telstra's CEO, Andy Penn, decided to make the company more customer-focused, fast-paced, and agile, he and his chief human resources officer, Alex Badenoch, dramatically flattened its hierarchy, reducing the number of organizational layers to three.

Penn, Badenoch, and their team recognized that the restructuring provided a perfect opportunity to redesign the managerial job. "This change has been needed for so long," Badenoch told us. "We realized we had to separate work and management and create two distinct roles: *leader of people* and *leader of work*." With very few exceptions, this new model applies to the entire organization.

Leaders of people are responsible for similarly skilled employees grouped into guildlike "chapters"—one for financial planners, say, and another for people experienced in change implementation. Most chapters consist of several hundred people, but some are larger. Subchapter leaders one level below are responsible for 15 to 20 members with narrower specializations and are located all over the world. What people do—not where they are—is what matters most.

Leaders of people ensure that the employees in their chapters have the skills and capabilities to meet the current and future needs of the business. They also help chapter members develop pathways to other chapters, to broaden insights and avoid silos. "The role of leaders of people," Badenoch told us, "is to know

> ## Telstra's Dual Manager Model
>
> To better cope with what it calls the new "equation of work," the telecommunications firm Telstra has flattened its hierarchy and split the traditional role of manager into two jobs: one devoted to people and the other to process. The two types of managers are equals and coordinate closely with each other.
>
> | Leader of people | Leader of work |
> |---|---|
> | Leads a global chapter of employees with similar skills | Leads an agile project team drawn from chapters and external contractors |
> | Owns the talent capacity, including personnel budgets | Owns the work, including project plans and budgets |
> | Forecasts skills gaps and closes them through training and hiring | Forecasts demand for skills |
> | Selects employees for projects | Bids for employees |
> | Is responsible for employee engagement, career movement, and skills | Is responsible for project deliverables and business outcomes |

people beyond their work, to understand their career aspirations, to feed their minds and create thought provocations." Their performance is judged by such standards as how engaged they are with the people on their teams (measured by Net Promoter Scores) and how well they fulfill requirements, among them the amount of time that their people are actively at work on projects, as opposed to "on the bench."

Leaders of work focus on the flow of work and the commercial imperatives of the business. They don't directly manage people or control operating budgets. Instead, they create and execute work plans and determine which chapters to draw from for them. These leaders' performance is judged by such standards as the clarity of their planning, the quality of their estimates, and whether their projects are on time and on budget.

This bold experiment has been widely acclaimed internally. "You actually get two people out of it who are dedicated to your development," one employee commented. "Your chapter lead [leader of people] is there to talk to you about your growth, and you get to have some great, powerful conversations about the type of work you want to do and how to get there. You can be very honest and share your aspirations openly with them. They have an amazing network and can get you assignments that allow you to explore different roles. And your project leader [leader of work] is there on a day-to-day basis to provide you direction on the work you need to do and on the business outcomes that we're trying to deliver."

At Telstra neither group of leaders is subordinate to the other. Their pay ranges are the same, and they participate as equals in the senior leadership team. Together they determine what Badenoch calls "the equation of work," which reveals "who is performing well, and what the skill and capacity is." Leaders of people have a sense of the dynamics of their talent pool, and leaders of work have a sense of the dynamics of workflow. By coordinating with their counterparts, leaders of people can anticipate skills gaps and prioritize training investments, or forecast undercapacity and the need for hiring—all while being mindful of the commitments, health, and well-being of employees.

This bifurcated model of management isn't new. It's been used for years in consulting, where one often finds a division between practice leadership and project leadership. What is new here is the context. Telstra has proven that the model can work effectively and profitably across all functions in big companies that have adopted agile practices and flexible work arrangements.

. . .

Let's step back and consider where we are. For roughly a century our approach to management was conventionally hierarchical. That made sense because work was organized sequentially and in silos, jobs were fixed, workspaces were physical, and information flowed downward. But that's no longer the case. In today's world of work, enabled by digitization, we prioritize agility, innovation, responsiveness, speed, and the value of human connection. All of that demands the new approach to management that we've discussed: one that involves shifts in power, skills, and structure.

We have to get this right. At no time in the past has the investor community paid such close attention to human capital in corporations—checking Glassdoor for signals of toxic work environments, demanding disclosure of metrics such as diversity and employee turnover. As the stewards of culture, managers are the lifeblood of organizations. The current state of overwhelmed, confused, and underskilled managers creates significant risk, not just to productivity and employee well-being but also to brand reputation.

Sometimes it takes a jolt like the new titles at Telstra and Standard Chartered, or the Manager Success Index at IBM, to signal that change is afoot. But in all cases the march to sustainable behavioral change is long. The Telstra experience shows us the benefits of a radical new organizational design, and the Standard Chartered and IBM experiences show us that at a minimum companies can take deliberate steps to shift managers' mindsets, energy, and focus. With these kinds of actions—which institutionalize change—we can ensure that people get the leadership they need in the new world of work.

Originally published in March–April 2022. Reprint R2202F

10

Are You a Good Boss—or a Great One?

by Linda A. Hill and Kent Lineback

"Am I good enough?"

"Am I ready? This is my big opportunity, but now I'm not sure I'm prepared."

These thoughts plagued Jason, an experienced manager, as he lay awake one night fretting about a new position he'd taken. For more than five years he had run a small team of developers in Boston. They produced two highly successful lines of engineering textbooks for the education publishing arm of a major media conglomerate. On the strength of his reputation as a great manager of product development, he'd been chosen by the company to take over an online technical-education startup based in London.

Jason arrived at his new office on a Monday morning, excited and confident, but by the end of his first week he was beginning to wonder whether he was up to the challenge. In his previous work he had led people who'd worked together before and required coordination but little supervision. There were problems, of course, but nothing like what he'd discovered in this new venture. Key members of his group barely talked to one another. Other publishers in the company, whose materials and collaboration he desperately needed, angrily viewed his new group as competition. The goals he'd been set seemed impossible—the group was about to miss some early milestones—and a crucial partnership with an outside organization had been badly, perhaps irretrievably, damaged. On top of all that, his boss, who was located in New York, offered little help. "That's why you're there" was the typical response whenever Jason described a problem. By Friday he was worried about living up to the expectations implied in that response.

Do Jason's feelings sound familiar? Such moments of doubt and even fear may and often do come despite years of management experience. Any number of events can trigger them: An initiative you're running isn't going as expected. Your people aren't performing as they should. You hear talk in the group that "the real problem here is lack of leadership." You think you're doing fine until you, like Jason, receive a daunting new assignment. You're given a lukewarm performance review. Or one day you simply realize that you're no longer growing and advancing—you're stuck.

Most Managers Stop Working on Themselves

The whole question of how managers grow and advance is one we've studied, thought about, and lived with for years. As a professor working with high potentials, MBAs, and executives from around the globe, Linda meets people who want to contribute to their organizations and build fulfilling careers. As an executive, Kent has worked with managers at all levels of both private and public organizations. All our experience brings us to a simple but

Idea in Brief

Many managers underestimate the transformational challenges of their roles—or they become complacent and stop growing and improving. At best they learn to get by; at worst they become terrible bosses. Sometimes even the best of them suffer doubts and fears despite years of management experience.

Three imperatives can guide managers on their journey to becoming great bosses: (1) Manage yourself. Productive influence comes from people's trust in your competence and character. (2) Manage your network. The organization as a whole must be engaged to create the conditions for your own and your team's success. (3) Manage your team. Effective managers forge a high-performing "we" out of all the individuals who report to them.

Constant and probing self-assessment across these three imperatives is essential, the authors write. They include a useful assessment tool to help readers get started.

---

troubling observation: Most bosses reach a certain level of proficiency and stop there—short of what they could and should be.

We've discussed this observation with countless colleagues, who almost without exception have seen what we see: Organizations usually have a few great managers, some capable ones, a horde of mediocre ones, some poor ones, and some awful ones. The great majority of people we work with are well-intentioned, smart, accomplished individuals. Many progress and fulfill their ambitions. But too many derail and fail to live up to their potential. Why? Because they stop working on themselves.

Managers rarely ask themselves, "How good am I?" and "Do I need to be better?" unless they're shocked into it. When did *you* last ask those questions? On the spectrum of great to awful bosses, where do you fall?

Managers in new assignments usually start out receptive to change. The more talented and ambitious ones choose stretch assignments, knowing that they'll have much to learn at first. But as they settle in and lose their fear of imminent failure, they often grow complacent. Every organization has its ways of doing things—policies, standard practices, and unspoken guidelines, such as "promote by seniority" and "avoid conflict." Once they're learned, managers often use them to get by—to "manage" in the worst sense of the word.

It doesn't help that a majority of the organizations we see offer their managers minimal support and rarely press the experienced ones to improve. Few expect more of their leaders than short-term results, which by themselves don't necessarily indicate real management skill.

In our experience, however, the real culprit is neither managerial complacency nor organizational failure: It is a lack of understanding. When bosses are questioned, it's clear that many of them have stopped making progress because they simply *don't know how to*.

Do you understand what's required to become truly effective?

Too often managers underestimate how much time and effort it takes to keep growing and developing. Becoming a great boss is a lengthy, difficult process of learning and change, driven mostly by personal experience. Indeed, so much time and effort are required that you can think of the process as a journey—a journey of years.

What makes the journey especially arduous is that the lessons involved cannot be taught. Leadership is using yourself as an instrument to get things done in the organization, so it is about self-development. There are no secrets and few shortcuts. You and every other manager must learn the lessons yourself, based on your own experience as a boss. If you don't understand the nature of the journey, you're more likely to pause or lose hope and tell yourself, "I can't do this" or "I'm good enough already."

Do you understand what you're trying to attain?

We all know how disorganized, fragmented, and even chaotic every manager's workdays are. Given this reality, which is intensifying as work and organizations become more complex and fluid, how can you as a boss do anything more than cope with what comes at you day by day?

To deal with the chaos, you need a clear underlying sense of what's important and where you and your group want to be in the future. You need a mental model that you can lay over the chaos and into which you can fit all the messy pieces as they come at you. This way of thinking begins with a straightforward definition: Management is responsibility for the performance of a group of people.

It's a simple idea, yet putting it into practice is difficult, because management is *defined* by responsibility but *done* by exerting influence. To influence others you must make a difference not only in what they do but also in the thoughts and feelings that drive their actions. How do you actually do this?

To answer that question, you need an overarching, integrated way of thinking about your work as a manager. We offer an approach based on studies of management practice, our own observations, and our knowledge of where managers tend to go wrong. We call it the *three imperatives:* Manage yourself. Manage your network. Manage your team.

Is this the only way to describe management? No, of course not. But it's clear, straightforward, and, above all, focused on what managers must actually do. People typically think of "management" as just the third imperative, but today all three are critical to success. Together they encompass the crucial activities that effective managers must perform to influence others. Mastering them is the purpose of your journey.

Manage Yourself

Management begins with you, because who you are as a person, what you think and feel, the beliefs and values that drive your actions, and especially how you connect with others all matter to the people you must influence. Every day those people examine every interaction with you, your every word and deed, to uncover your intentions. They ask themselves, "Can I trust this person?" How hard they work, their level of personal commitment, their willingness to accept your influence, will depend in large part on the qualities they see in you. And their perceptions will determine the answer to this fundamental question every manager must ask: Am I someone who can influence others productively?

Who you are shows up most clearly in the relationships you form with others, especially those for whom you're responsible. It's easy to get those crucial relationships wrong. Effective managers possess the self-awareness and self-management required to get them right.

José, a department head, told us of two managers who worked for him in the marketing department of a large maker of durable goods. Both managers were struggling to deliver the results expected of their groups. Both, it turned out, were creating dysfunctional relationships. One was frankly ambivalent about being "the boss" and hated it when people referred to him that way. He wanted to be liked, so he tried to build close personal relationships. He would say, in effect, "Do what I ask because we're friends." That worked for a while until, for good reasons, he had to turn down one "friend" for promotion and deny another one a bonus. Naturally, those people felt betrayed, and their dissatisfaction began to poison the feelings of everyone else in the group.

The other manager took the opposite approach. With her it was all business. No small talk or reaching out to people as people. For her, results mattered, and she'd been made the boss because she was the one who knew what needed to be done; it was the job of her people to execute. Not surprisingly, her message was always "Do what I say because I'm the boss." She was effective—until people began leaving.

If productive influence doesn't arise from being liked ("I'm your friend!") or from fear ("I'm the boss!"), where does it come from? From people's trust in you as a manager. That trust has two components: belief in your *competence* (you know what to do and how to do it) and belief in your *character* (your motives are good and you want your people to do well).

Trust is the foundation of all forms of influence other than coercion, and you need to conduct yourself with others in ways that foster it. Management really does begin with who you are as a person.

Manage Your Network

We once talked to Kim, the head of a software company division, just as he was leaving a meeting of a task force consisting of his peers. He had proposed a new way of handling interdivisional sales, which he believed would increase revenue by encouraging each division to cross-sell other divisions' products. At the meeting he'd made an extremely well-researched, carefully reasoned, and even compelling case for his proposal—which the group rejected with very little discussion. "How many of these people did you talk to about your proposal before the meeting?" we asked. None, it turned out. "But I anticipated all their questions and objections," he protested, adding with some bitterness, "It's just politics. If they can't see what's good for the company and them, I can't help them."

Many managers resist the need to operate effectively in their organizations' political environments. They consider politics dysfunctional—a sign the organization is broken—and don't realize that it unavoidably arises from three features inherent in all organizations: *division of labor,* which creates disparate groups with disparate and even conflicting goals and priorities; *interdependence,* which means that none of those groups can do their work without the others; and *scarce resources,* for which groups necessarily compete. Obviously, some organizations handle the politics better than others, but conflict and competition among groups are inevitable. How do they get resolved? Through organizational influence. Groups whose managers have influence tend to get what they need; other groups don't.

Unfortunately, many managers deal with conflict by trying to avoid it. "I hate company politics!" they say. "Just let me do my job." But effective managers know they cannot turn away. Instead, with integrity and for good ends, they proactively engage the organization to create the conditions for their success. They build and nurture a broad network of ongoing relationships with those they need and those who need them; that is how they influence people over whom they have no formal authority. They also take responsibility for making their boss, a key member of their network, a source of influence on their behalf.

Manage Your Team

As a manager, Wei worked closely with each of her people, who were spread across the U.S. and the Far East. But she rarely called a virtual group meeting, and only once had her group met face-to-face. "In my experience," she told us, "meetings online or in person are usually a waste of time. Some people do all the yakking, others stay silent, and not much gets done. It's a lot more efficient for me to work with each person and arrange for them to coordinate when that's necessary." It turned out, though, that she was spending all her time "coordinating," which included a great deal of conflict mediation. People under her seemed to be constantly at odds, vying for the scarce resources they needed to achieve their disparate goals and complaining about what others were or were not doing.

Too many managers overlook the possibilities of creating a real team and managing their people as a whole. They don't realize that managing one-on-one is just not the same as managing a group and that they can influence individual behavior much more effectively through the group, because most of us are social creatures who want to fit in and be accepted as part of the team. How do you make the people who work for you, whether on a project or permanently, into a real team—a group of people who are mutually committed to a common purpose and the goals related to that purpose?

To do collective work that requires varied skills, experience, and knowledge, teams are more creative and productive than groups of individuals who merely cooperate. In a real team, members hold themselves and one another jointly accountable. They share a genuine conviction that they will succeed or fail together. A clear and compelling purpose, and concrete goals and

Measuring yourself on the three imperatives

Are you performing all the activities necessary to be an effective boss? To get some sense of where you stand, assess yourself on the following questions:

			I need to make progress				This is a strength
Manage yourself	1. Do you use your formal authority effectively?	This is a strength if you consider it a useful tool but not your primary means of influencing others. You make clear why you do what you do—and even share your authority with others when possible and appropriate. You focus more on the responsibilities that come with authority than on the personal privileges it provides.	1	2	3	4	5
	2. Do you create thoughtful but not overly personal relationships?	This is a strength if your relationships are rich in human connections but always focused on the purpose and goals of the team and the organization. You avoid trying to influence people by befriending them.	1	2	3	4	5
	3. Do you exercise your influence ethically?	This is a strength if people, particularly your own, believe in your competence, intentions, and values. You demonstrate concern for their individual success.	1	2	3	4	5
	4. Do you exercise your influence ethically?	This is a strength if you consistently identify stakeholders, weigh their interests, and try to mitigate any harm that your actions may cause as you attempt to accomplish a greater good.	1	2	3	4	5

Manage your network	5. Do you systematically identify those who should be in your network?	This is a strength if you are always aware of which people and groups you and your team depend on, and vice versa, as circumstances change.	1	2	3	4	5
	6. Do you proactively build and maintain your network?	This is a strength if you create and sustain relationships with those in your network, connect frequently with them, and support their needs.	1	2	3	4	5
	7. Do you use your network to provide the protection and resources your team needs?	This is a strength if you protect your team from distractions and misunderstandings, use your network to solve problems inside and outside the team, and secure the funds, people, and other resources it needs.	1	2	3	4	5
	8. Do you use your network to accomplish your team's goals?	This is a strength if you form coalitions of network members to support your team's goals and help others in your network achieve theirs. Your network colleagues believe in your competence and character.	1	2	3	4	5

(continued)

Measuring yourself on the three imperatives (continued)

		I need to make progress			This is a strength	
Manage your team	9. Do you define and constantly refine your team's vision for the future?	This is a strength if you've defined your team's purpose and the goals, strategies, and actions that will take you there. You constantly gather information, discuss your plans with others, and refine your ideas.	1	2	3	4	5
	10. Do you clarify roles, work rules, team culture, and feedback about performance for your team?	This is a strength if your people feel a strong sense of "we"—that they're all pulling together toward the same worthwhile goals. They know how they individually contribute and what the team's work involves. They receive regular feedback from you.	1	2	3	4	5
	11. Do you know and manage your people as individuals as well as team members?	This is a strength if you interact equitably with all team members individually. You delegate, strive to help people grow, and constantly assess their performance. You hire people who both fit the team and add diversity, and you deal with performance issues quickly.	1	2	3	4	5
	12. Do you use daily activities and problems to pursue the three imperatives?	This is a strength if you regularly consider how every problem, obligation, or event can help you build your team, make progress on its goals, develop people, and strengthen your network.	1	2	3	4	5

How did you do? Did your responses cover the whole range from 1 to 5? If you consistently assessed yourself at 3 or above, you should be skeptical. In our experience, few bosses merit high ratings across the board. Did you give yourself mostly 3s? Take care not to hide in the middle, telling yourself, "I'm OK—not great, but not failing either." And don't be satisfied to stay there. "I'm not failing" is the watchword of those who are comfortable—and stuck.

plans based on that purpose, are critical. Without them no group will coalesce into a real team.

Team culture is equally important. Members need to know what's required of them collectively and individually; what the team's values, norms, and standards are; how members are expected to work together (what kind of conflict is acceptable or unacceptable, for example); and how they should communicate. It's your job to make sure they have all this crucial knowledge.

Effective managers also know that even in a cohesive team they cannot ignore individual members. Every person wants to be a valued member of a group *and* needs individual recognition. You must be able to provide the attention members need, but always in the context of the team.

And finally, effective managers know how to lead a team through the work it does day after day—including the unplanned problems and opportunities that frequently arise—to make progress toward achieving their own and the team's goals.

Be Clear on How You're Doing

The three imperatives will help you influence both those who work for you and those who don't. Most important, they provide a clear and actionable road map for your journey. You must master them to become a fully effective manager.

These imperatives are not simply distinct managerial competencies. They are tightly integrated activities, each of which depends on the others. Getting your person-to-person relationships right is critical to building a well-functioning team and giving its individual members the attention they need. A compelling team purpose, bolstered by clear goals and plans, is the foundation for a strong network, and a network is indispensable for reaching your team's goals.

Knowing where you're going is only the first half of what's required. You also need to know at all times where you are on your journey and what you must do to make progress. We're all aware that the higher you rise in an organization, the less feedback you get about your performance. You have to be prepared to regularly assess yourself.

Too many managers seem to assume that development happens automatically. They have only a vague sense of the goal and of where they stand in relation to it. They tell themselves, "I'm doing all right" or "As I take on more challenges, I'll get better." Consequently, those managers fall short. There's no substitute for routinely taking a look at yourself and how you're doing. (The exhibit "Measuring yourself on the three imperatives" will help you do this.)

Don't be discouraged if you find several areas in which you could do better. No manager will meet all the standards implicit in the three imperatives. The goal is not perfection. It's developing the strengths you need for success and compensating for any fatal shortcomings. Look at your strengths and weaknesses in the context of your organization. What knowledge and skills does it—or will it—need to reach its goals? How can your strengths help it move forward? Given its needs and priorities, what weaknesses must you address right away? The answers become your personal learning goals.

What You Can Do Right Now

Progress will come only from your work experience: from trying and learning, observing and interacting with others, experimenting, and sometimes pushing yourself beyond the bounds of comfort—and then assessing yourself on the three imperatives again and again. Above all, take responsibility for your own development; ultimately, all development is self-development.

You won't make progress unless you consciously act. Before you started a business, you would draw up a business plan broken into manageable steps with milestones; do the same as you think about your journey. Set personal goals. Solicit feedback from others. Take advantage of company training programs. Create a network of trusted advisers, including role models and mentors. Use your strengths to seek out developmental experiences. We know you've heard all this advice before, and it is good advice. But what we find most effective is building the learning into your daily work.

For this purpose we offer a simple approach we call *prep, do, review*.

Prep

Begin each morning with a quick preview of the coming day's events. For each one, ask yourself how you can use it to develop as a manager and in particular how you can work on your specific learning goals. Consider delegating a task you would normally take on yourself and think about how you might do that—to whom, what questions you should ask, what boundaries or limits you should set, what preliminary coaching you might provide. Apply the same thinking during the day when a problem comes up unexpectedly. Before taking any action, step back and consider how it might help you become better. Stretch yourself. If you don't move outside familiar patterns and practice new approaches, you're unlikely to learn.

Do

Take whatever action is required in your daily work, and as you do, use the new and different approaches you planned. Don't lose your resolve. For example, if you tend to cut off conflict in a meeting, even constructive conflict, force yourself to hold back so that disagreement can be expressed and worked through. Step in only if the discussion becomes personal or points of view are being stifled. The ideas that emerge may lead you to a better outcome.

Review

After the action, examine what you did and how it turned out. This is where learning actually occurs. Reflection is critical, and it works best if you make it a regular practice. For example, set aside time toward the end of each day—perhaps on your commute home. Which actions worked well? What might you have done differently? Replay conversations. Compare what you did with what you might have done if you were the manager you aspire to be. Where did you disappoint yourself, and how did that happen? Did you practice any new behaviors or otherwise make progress on your journey?

Some managers keep notes about how they spent their time, along with thoughts about what they learned. One CEO working on a corporate globalization strategy told us he'd started recording every Friday his reflections about the past week. Within six weeks, he said, he'd developed greater discipline to say no to anything "not on the critical path," which gave him time to spend with key regulators and to jump-start the strategy.

If you still need to make progress on your journey, that should spur you to action, not discourage you. You can become what you want and need to be. But you must take personal responsibility for mastering the three imperatives and assessing where you are now.

Originally published in January–February 2011. Reprint R1101K

Discussion Guide

Are you feeling inspired by what you've read in this collection? Do you want to share the ideas in the articles or explore the insights you've gleaned with others? This discussion guide offers an opportunity to dig a little deeper, with questions to prompt personal reflection and to start conversations with your team.

You don't need to have read the book from beginning to end to use this guide. Choose the questions that apply to the articles you have read or that you feel might spark the liveliest discussion.

Reflect on key takeaways from your reading to help you adopt the ideas and techniques you want to integrate into your work as a leader. What tools can you share with your team to help everyone be their best? Becoming the leader you want to be starts with a detailed plan—and a commitment to carrying it out.

1. What does it mean to you to manage people? Did you aspire to be a manager or did the role find you as you moved up?

2. Which of Daniel Goleman's six leadership styles (coercive, authoritative, affiliative, democratic, pacesetting, and coaching) do you excel at and which would you like to develop further? How does your approach affect the climate, morale, and productivity of your team? Discuss these questions with your team. Do you have a good balance of styles represented?

3. How do you currently acknowledge and celebrate small wins with your team? What catalysts and nourishers

might help team members make consistent progress in their work? What strategies would minimize progress inhibitors and toxins? How can you strengthen the connection between individual work and organizational purpose?

4. How can you foster a coaching culture with your people, where continuous learning and development are prioritized? How can you integrate ongoing development into everyday meetings and practices? What metrics would help you assess whether your coaching efforts produce tangible improvements in performance and engagement?

5. How can you support team members when they're entrusted with significant decisions, ensuring they have the necessary resources and guidance to succeed? (If it's helpful, consider when something important was delegated to you and what forms of support were or were not offered.) How does your team handle situations when delegated decisions lead to unexpected outcomes or failures? What processes are in place to learn from these experiences and improve future decision-making?

6. Can you think of an example of the set-up-to-fail syndrome on display—when tightening controls on a poor performer resulted in even poorer performance and loss of motivation? What mechanisms could you put in place to ensure that you don't reinforce in-group and out-group membership on your team? What resources or support systems could you implement to assist people who are struggling without triggering the set-up-to-fail syndrome's vicious cycle?

7. How do you prioritize tasks when people are assigned to multiple projects simultaneously? When conflicts arise between projects, what criteria do you use to determine which assignments take precedence? What measures could you implement to prevent overcommitment and burnout—for yourself and others?

8. How do cultural differences influence your global team's interactions? (If your team isn't global, consider how these questions might apply to hybrid work or other types of difference instead.) Of the elements in Tsedal Neeley's SPLIT framework for managing the social distance that afflicts dispersed teams, which is most problematic for your team: structure, process, language, identity, or technology? (Or rank all five in order of most to least problematic.) Which strategies for building emotional connection and trust do you think could work for you and your people?

9. What are the most common types of conflict that arise within your team? What targeted strategies might help you resolve the type of conflict you see most, whether it's conflict caused by a solo dissenter, a boxing match between two teammates, warring factions, or whole-team discord? Which types of conflict can actually benefit the team, if handled properly?

10. How could you improve the match between teammates' job descriptions and their goals and provide clear pathways for career growth and development within the organization? Think about the push-and-pull factors your people might be experiencing.

11. Can you think of times in your own career when you received feedback on what you did well and other times when your shortcomings were emphasized? Which was most helpful and inspiring? Who delivered the most useful advice—a boss, a peer, or someone else you admire? What *can* you do as a manager to help support people's learning and generate truly excellent performance?

12. How do you think the people on your team would describe the current level of psychological safety? What specific actions can you take (individually and as a team) to create an environment where diverse perspectives are actively sought, valued, and harnessed to power exceptional team performance? How can you monitor levels of psychological safety and ensure that adjustments are made to team culture as needed?

13. What benefits and drawbacks would you expect to see from splitting the managerial role into two parts—leader of people and leader of work—as the authors of "Managers Can't Do It All" suggest? Do you think you would excel in one role or the other? How would people in your organization respond to this idea?

14. According to Linda Hill and Kent Lineback, what separates good bosses from great ones? Where are you on your management journey right now and what do you need to focus on to make progress? What knowledge and skills are needed to help your organization reach its goals and which of your weaknesses should be addressed right away, given organizational priorities? (Answer the questions in the article sidebar, "Measuring Yourself on the Three

Imperatives" for a detailed road map of your strengths and weaknesses as a manager.)

15. What other sources on managing people have had a significant impact on your work? Were there voices or subtopics you missed in this collection? Were there voices or subtopics included that surprised you?

16. After reading and reflecting on this book and discussing it with people on your team, write down the ideas and techniques you want to try. Think of how you might experiment and implement them in both the short term and long term. Draft a plan to move forward.

Notes

Chapter 4: The Set-Up-to-Fail Syndrome

1. The influence of expectations on performance has been observed in numerous experiments by Dov Eden and his colleagues. See Dov Eden, "Leadership and Expectations: Pygmalion Effects and Other Self-Fulfilling Prophecies in Organizations," *Leadership Quarterly*, Winter 1992, vol. 3, no. 4, pp. 271–305.

2. Chris Argyris has written extensively on how and why people tend to behave unproductively in situations they see as threatening or embarrassing. See, for example, *Knowledge for Action: A Guide to Overcoming Barriers to Organizational Change* (San Francisco: Jossey-Bass, 1993).

Quick Read: Four Types of Team Conflict—and How to Resolve Them

1. CPP Global, "Human Capital Report: Workplace Conflict and How Businesses Can Harness It to Thrive," July 2008, https://img.en25.com/Web/CPP/Conflict_report.pdf.

2. Priti Pradhan Shah, Randall S. Peterson, and Amanda J. Ferguson, "Things Are Not Always What They Seem: The Origins and Evolution of Intragroup Conflict," *Administrative Science Quarterly* 66, no. 2 (October 10, 2020), https://journals.sagepub.com/doi/10.1177/0001839220965186.

3. Shah et al., "Things Are Not Always What They Seem."

4. Charlan Nemeth, *In Defense of Troublemakers: The Power of Dissent in Life and Business* (New York: Hachette Book Group, 2018).

5. Shah et al., "Things Are Not Always What They Seem."

6. Roger Fisher, William L. Ury, and Bruce Patton, *Getting to Yes: Negotiating Agreement Without Giving In* (New York: Penguin Random House, 2011).

7. Shah et al., "Things Are Not Always What They Seem."

Quick Read: To Excel, Diverse Teams Need Psychological Safety

1. Deborah Sole and Amy Edmondson, "Situated Knowledge and Learning in Dispersed Teams," *British Journal of Management* 13, no. S2 (2002): S17–34, https:// doi.org/10.1111/1467-8551.13.s2.3, https://dash.harvard.edu/handle/1/37907101; Mar Yam G. Hamedani and Hazel Rose Markus, "Understanding Culture Clashes and Catalyzing Change: A Cultural Cycle Approach," *Frontiers in Psychology* 10 (2019), https://doi.org/10.3389/fpsyg.2019.00700.

2. Sujin K. Horwitz and Irwin B. Horwitz, "The Effects of Team Diversity on Team Outcomes: A Meta-Analytic Review of Team Demography," *Southern Management Association Journal of Management* 33 (2007), https://doi.org/10.1177/0149206307308587.
3. Henrik Bresman and Amy C. Edmondson, "Exploring the Relationship between Team Diversity, Psychological Safety and Team Performance: Evidence from Pharmaceutical Drug Development," Working Paper No. 22-055, Harvard Business School, Boston, February 2022.
4. Stephen Scott and Amy Edmondson, "Unlocking Diversity's Promise: Psychological Safety, Trust and Inclusion," Reuters, April 13, 2021, https://www.reuters.com/article/bc-finreg-unlocking-diversity-inclusion/unlocking-diversitys-promise-psychological-safety-trust-and-inclusion-idUSKBN2C01N2/; Amy Edmondson and Kathryn Roloff, "Leveraging Diversity Through Psychological Safety," in *Team Effectiveness in Complex Organizations: Cross-Disciplinary Perspectives and Approaches* (Milton Park, England: Routledge Academic, 2008), https://scholar.harvard.edu/files/afriberg/files/leveraging_diversity_through_psychological_safety_hbs_article.pdf.

About the Contributors

Teresa M. Amabile is the Edsel Bryant Ford Professor, Emerita, at Harvard Business School. A psychologist who has researched creativity, motivation, and everyday work life, she is a coauthor of *The Progress Principle* and *Retiring: Creating a Life That Works for You*.

Jean-Louis Barsoux is a term research professor at IMD and a coauthor of *ALIEN Thinking*.

Ethan Bernstein is the Edward W. Conard Associate Professor of Business Administration in the organizational behavior unit at Harvard Business School and a coauthor of *Job Moves*.

Henrik Bresman is an associate professor of organizational behavior at INSEAD. He is a coauthor of the book *X-Teams, Updated* (Harvard Business Review Press, 2023).

Marcus Buckingham is a researcher of high performance at work and a cocreator of StrengthsFinder and StandOut. He is a coauthor of *Nine Lies About Work* and the author of *Love + Work* (both from Harvard Business Review Press).

Amy C. Edmondson is the Novartis Professor of Leadership and Management at Harvard Business School. She is the author of the book *Right Kind of Wrong*.

About the Contributors

Amanda J. Ferguson is an associate professor of management at Northern Illinois University, where she teaches classes on organizational behavior and leading teams.

Sydney Finkelstein is the Steven Roth Professor of Management at the Tuck School of Business at Dartmouth College, the author of *The Superbosses Playbook*, and the host of *The Sydcast* podcast. You can follow him on X/Twitter @sydfinkelstein.

Heidi K. Gardner is a distinguished fellow at Harvard Law School; the author of multiple books, including *Smarter Collaboration* (Harvard Business Review Press, 2022); and the CEO of the research and advisory firm Gardner & Co.

Diane Gherson is the former chief human resources officer of IBM, a director of Kraft Heinz, and a senior adviser at Boston Consulting Group.

Daniel Goleman, best known for his writing on emotional intelligence, is codirector of the Consortium for Research on Emotional Intelligence in Organizations at Rutgers University. He offers training on emotional intelligence competencies through Emotional Intelligence Training Programs online. He is the author of several books, including *Primal Leadership*, *Altered Traits*, and *Building Blocks of Emotional Intelligence*.

Ashley Goodall is a leadership expert who has spent his career exploring large organizations from the inside, most recently as an executive at Cisco. He is a coauthor of *Nine Lies About Work*, which was selected as the best management book of 2019 by *strategy+business* and as one of Amazon's best business and leadership books of 2019. Prior to Cisco, he spent 14 years at Deloitte as a consultant and as the chief learning officer for leadership and professional development. His latest book is *The Problem with Change*.

Lynda Gratton is a professor of management practice at London Business School and the founder of HSM Advisory, a future-of-work research consultancy. She is the author of the book *Redesigning Work*.

Linda A. Hill is the Wallace Brett Donham Professor of Business Administration and faculty chair of the Leadership Initiative at Harvard Business School, the author of *Becoming a Manager*, and a coauthor of *Being the Boss* and *Collective Genius* (all from Harvard Business Review Press).

Michael B. Horn is a cofounder of and a distinguished fellow at the Clayton Christensen Institute. He teaches at the Harvard Graduate School of Education and cohosts the higher ed podcast *Future U*.

Herminia Ibarra is the Charles Handy Professor of Organisational Behaviour at London Business School and the author of *Act Like a Leader, Think Like a Leader, Updated* and *Working Identity, Updated* (both from Harvard Business Review Press, 2023).

Stephen L. Jones is an associate professor of management at the University of Washington Bothell, where he teaches organizational and strategic management.

About the Contributors

Steven J. Kramer is an independent researcher, writer, and consultant based in Wayland, Massachusetts. He is a coauthor of *The Progress Principle* and *Creativity at Work*.

Kent Lineback spent many years as a manager and an executive in business and government. He is a coauthor of *Collective Genius* (Harvard Business Review Press, 2014).

Jean-François Manzoni was, for eight years, the president of IMD, where he is a professor of leadership, organizational development, and corporate governance.

Bob Moesta is the CEO and founder of The Re-Wired Group, an adjunct lecturer at the Kellogg School of Management, and a research fellow at the Clayton Christensen Institute.

Mark Mortensen is a professor of organizational behavior at INSEAD and for over 20 years has studied and consulted on collaboration and organization design, with a focus on hybrid, virtual, and globally distributed work. His work has appeared in *Harvard Business Review*, *MIT Sloan Management Review*, *INSEAD Knowledge*, the *Economist*, the *Financial Times*, and *Fortune*, and on the BBC.

Tsedal Neeley is the Naylor Fitzhugh Professor of Business Administration and senior associate dean of faculty and research at Harvard Business School. She is a coauthor of the book *The Digital Mindset* (Harvard Business Review Press, 2022) and the author of the book *Remote Work Revolution*.

About the Contributors

Randall S. Peterson is the academic director of the Leadership Institute and a professor of organizational behavior at London Business School, where he teaches leadership in the Senior Executive and Accelerated Development Program.

Anne Scoular is a cofounder of Meyler Campbell, which trains senior leaders to coach. She is also an associate scholar at the University of Oxford's Saïd Business School and the author of *The Financial Times Guide to Business Coaching*.

Priti Pradhan Shah is a professor in the Department of Work and Organization at the Carlson School of Management at the University of Minnesota, where she teaches negotiation in the Executive Education and MBA Programs.

Index

accountability
   delegating and, 78
   democratic leadership and, 17
   leadership styles and, 24–25
   pacesetting leadership and, 19
   in teams, 117, 119
accreditation, for managers, 214, 215, 216
affiliative leaders, 3, 11, 14–16, 25
agile movement, 211
alignment, job switches for, 163, 164
Allen & Overy, 65, 71–73
Amabile, Teresa M., 33–54
Apple, 43
assumptions
   in global teams, 139–141
   psychological safety and, 199–200
   in set-up-to-fail syndrome, 81–93, 106–108
attribution bias, 95–96
attrition, cost of, 159–160
authoritative leaders, 2, 10, 11–14, 26
authority
   agile movement and, 211
   coaching and, 58
   delegation and, 76, 78–79
   self-management and, 228, 232
   set-up-to-fail syndrome and, 88
awareness, of employees' inner work life, 53. *See also* self-awareness

Badenoch, Alex, 218–219, 220, 221
Ballmer, Steve, 68
banking, management models in, 213–215
Barry, Rick, 191
Barsoux, Jean-Louis, 81–108

belonging, affiliative leadership and, 14–15
Berkeley Partnership, 65, 67
Bernstein, Ethan, 157–180
"best days" vs. "worst days," 38–41
biases
   attribution, 95–96
   source of truth and, 184–187
blame game, 153–154
"blind men and elephant problem," 113–115
boundaries
   around delegation, 78–79
   bridging, 204–205
boxing matches, in team conflict, 150–152
brain
   development of, 188–190
   emotional intelligence and, 29–30
brainstorming, 137
Bresman, Henrik, 199–206
Bridgewater Associates, 181, 182
Brinker, Norman, 75, 76–77
Brosius, Scott, 15
Buckingham, Marcus, 181–198
Burger King, 76–77
burnout, 114–115, 207–222
business movements, 210–213

Camus, Albert, 93
Carver, Joe, 170
catalysts, 38–41, 46–48
categorical thinking, 89–90, 107–108
change, leadership styles and, 23
character, 229

check-ins, 52
  in global teams, 134
  multiteaming and, 120, 125
Chiat, Jay, 76
Christensen, Clayton, 164
climate
  authoritative leadership and, 13
  coercive leadership and, 9
  leadership behaviors and, 6–8
  pacesetting leadership and, 19
  supporting progress and, 48–49
closure, premature, 89–90
coaching
  aspiration vs. practice and, 58–59
  barriers to, 70–71
  collateral benefits of, 65, 67
  definition of, 57–59
  developing ability in, 58–66
  developing leaders into, 214–215
  GROW model for, 64–66
  leadership style, 3, 11, 20–23, 25
  leaders in, 55–73
  matrix on, 62–64
  modeling and, 67–69
  as organizational capacity, 66–74
  resources on, 72
  self-assessment of, 61–62
coercive leaders, 2, 8–11
color blindness, 185–186
command-and-control style, 56, 69–71
commitment
  coaching leadership style and, 22–23
  coercive leadership and, 9
  democratic leadership and, 17
  leadership styles and, 25
  pacesetting leadership and, 19
communication
  affiliative leadership and, 15–16
  emotional intelligence and, 27–30
  in global teams, 137–139
  global teams and, 129–130, 139–144
  job descriptions and, 173–175
  listening and, 66, 169, 204–205
  multimodal/redundant, 143–144
  multiteaming and, 120–121
  psychological safety for, 199–206
  set-up-to-fail and, 101, 108
  set-up-to-fail syndrome and, 101–104
  unstructured time for, 135, 137
competence, 229
conflict
  blame game in, 153–154
  boxing matches, 150–152
  global teams and, 137
  solo dissenters and, 148–150
  tailoring your approach to, 154–155
  in teams, 147–155
  warring factions in, 152–153
consensus, 17–18
control, job switches for, 163, 164
coordination costs, 115
cost management, multiteaming and, 110, 112
Courtois, Jean-Phillipe, 69–71
Covid-19 pandemic, 159
Craig, Kyle, 76–77
creativity
  inner work life and, 35, 37
  meaningful work and, 43
Crick, Francis, 33–34
culture
  global teams and, 129–145
  knowledge transfer and, 126
  language differences and, 136
  at Microsoft, 69–74
  multiteaming and, 125
  psychological safety and, 199–206
  in teams, 234
curiosity, 121

Dallas Cowboys, 193
decision-making
  coercive leadership and, 9
  delegating, 75–79

Index

democratic leadership and, 17–18
  setting boundaries around, 78–79
  set-up-to-fail syndrome and, 83, 85
defensiveness, 92–93
delegation, 75–79
democratic leaders, 3, 11, 16–18, 30
digitization, 211
directive coaching, 62–63
divergent thinking, 149–150
diversity
  conflict and, 151–152
  employee desire for, 221
  global teams and, 129–145
  job switches and, 158
  psychological safety and, 199–206
division of labor, 230–231
The Double Helix (Watson), 33–34
Dweck, Carol, 68
dyadic conflict, 150–152

Edmondson, Amy C., 199–206
Ellison, Larry, 75
email, 142, 143
emotional intelligence
  business results and, 3–8
  definition of, 4
  effective leadership styles and, 2–31
  growing your, 28–30
  leadership styles and, 27, 30
  primer on, 4–5
emotional investment, 108
emotions
  inner work life and, 38, 40
  set-up-to-fail syndrome and, 93–94
  social distance and, 130–145
  source of truth on, 186–187
empathy, 27, 30
  employee interviews and, 168
  global teams and, 134–137
  perspective-taking and, 149–150
employees
  commitment and, 109–128
  cost of replacing, 104–105
  knowing and delegating to, 77–78
  why they quit, 157–180
empowerment, 93
  delegating and, 75–79
  global teams and, 138–139, 140
  management models and, 213
  monitoring employees and, 106–107
engagement
  in global teams, 138–139
  managers and, 210, 216
  set-up-to-fail syndrome and, 92
  in teams, 115–123
equation of work, 220, 221
excellence, theory of, 184, 190–192
exit interviews, 167–170, 191
expectations
  job switches and, 167, 176
  set-up-to-fail syndrome and, 81–108
  for teams, 117, 118, 121, 122
experimentation, 76–78
expertise, 55–56
  bridging boundaries in, 204–205
  multiteaming and, 112

failure, excellence and, 191–192
fairness, 105–106, 123
fear, influence and, 229
Fearn, Mark, 67
feedback, 181–198
  affiliative leadership and, 14
  in global teams, 135
  helping people excel with, 192–197
  multiteaming and, 120–121
  pacesetting leadership and, 19
  past, present, and future in, 196–197

Index

feedback (*continued*)
  in performance development, 217–218
  progress loop and, 54
  on routine interactions in global teams, 135
  set-up-to-fail and, 97–100
  specificity in, 194
  systematic error in, 185–187
  theory of excellence and, 184, 190–192
  theory of learning and, 183, 187–190
  theory of the source of truth and, 182–183
  as unalloyed good, 182–184
  working climate and, 6–8
Ferguson, Amanda J., 147–155
fight-or-flight response, 164, 189
Finkelstein, Sydney, 75–79
flexibility
  affiliative leadership and, 14
  among leadership styles, 23–26
  coaching leadership style and, 22
  coercive leadership and, 9
  global teams and, 144–145
  job switches for, 164
  multiteaming and, 113
  pacesetting leadership and, 19
  in teams, 115–123
  working climate and, 6–8
flexible work movement, 211–213
fluency gap, 136, 137–139
Fontaine, Mary, 6
framing, 202–203

Gardner, Heidi K., 109–128
Gherson, Diane, 207–222
gig economy, 113
Glassdoor, 221
goals
  coaching and, 64
  global teams and, 133–134
  meaningful work and, 43, 45
  of multiteaming, 122
  personal learning, 235–236
  set-up-to-fail and, 99–101
  for teams, 234–235
Goleman, Daniel, 1–31, 60
Goodall, Ashley, 181–198
GrainCorp, 179
Gratton, Lynda, 207–222
GROW model, 64–66
growth mindset, 68–69

Hanigan, Maury, 172
happiness, progress and, 40
Hay/McBer, 2, 6
help, set-up-to-fail syndrome and asking for, 92
Herzberg, Frederick, 36
Hill, Linda A., 223–237
Holacracy, 177–178
Horn, Michael B., 157–180
HR. *See* human resources (HR)
human capital, 221
human capital interdependencies, 123–125
human resources (HR), 175–179, 216

Ibarra, Herminia, 55–73
IBM, 208, 215–218, 221–222
identity
  in global teams, 139–142
  global teams and, 132–134
  multiteaming and, 121
idiosyncratic rater effect, 185
IDRsolutions, 176
inclusion, in global teams, 139
influence, 227–228, 229, 233–235
in-groups, 88–90
inhibitors, 39–41, 46
inner work life effect, 36–41
innovation
  affiliative leadership and, 14
  coaching and, 56

global teams and, 145
at IBM, 215–216
multiteaming and, 123, 130
psychological safety and, 199, 200, 204–205
small wins and, 33
inquiry, psychological safety and, 204–205
instruction, 182
interdependencies
in human capital, 123–125
work politics and, 230–231
internal mobility, 178
interrupts, highest-priority, 195–196
interviews, employee, 165, 166–171

Jacobs, Ruth, 6
job application process, 171–175
job descriptions, 165–166, 171–175
Jobs, Steve, 43
job satisfaction
motivation and, 36
psychological safety and, 201–202
jobs to be done theory, 164
job switches
interviews and, 166–171
push and pull factors in, 160–163, 166–171
quests for progress in, 163–166
Jones, Stephen L., 147–155
judgmental climate, 49

Kaplan, Robert Steven, 137–138
Kline, Nancy, 66
knowledge, reflected, 135
knowledge transfer, multiteaming and, 124–126
Kramer, Steven J., 33–54

labeling, 88–90
laissez-faire coaching, 61

Landry, Tom, 193
language differences, 135, 136, 137–139
feedback and, 194–195
leaders and leadership
art vs. science of, 30–31
of people, 218–219
styles for effective, 1–31
of work, 218, 219–220
working climate and, 6
leadership styles, 1–31
affiliative, 3, 14–16
authoritative, 2–3, 10, 11–14
climate and, 6–8
coaching, 3, 20–23
coaching and, 58
coercive, 2, 8–11
democratic, 3, 16–18
expanding your repertory of, 26–30
pacesetting, 3, 18–20
using various, 23–26
learning
coaching and, 56
coaching matrix and, 60–62
feedback and, 181–198
global teams and, 140–142
at Microsoft, 68–71
multiteaming and, 120–121
ongoing, 223–237
personal goals for, 234–235
teams and, 117–119
theory of, 183, 187–190
LeDoux, Joseph, 188
Lineback, Kent, 223–237
LinkedIn, 173–174
listening
coaching and, 66
in employee interviews, 169
psychological safety and, 204–205
Litwin, George, 6–8
loyalty, 14
Lucas, George, 78
Lucasfilm, 78

managers and management
  accreditation for, 214, 215, 216
  business movements and, 210–213
  discussion guide on, 239–243
  managing yourself and, 222–229
  need for, 210
  network management and, 229–230, 233
  new models of, 213–221
  ongoing learning for, 223–237
  as people leaders, 212, 213, 218–219
  professional development of, 235–237
  struggle of to keep up, 207–222
  of teams, 231–234
  three imperatives for, 228, 232
Manzoni, Jean-François, 81–108
matrix, coaching, 60–62
McClelland, David, 3, 6
McKinsey, 116, 210
meaningful work
  employee retention and, 158
  how managers strip meaning from, 44–45
  progress, motivation, and, 42–45
  supporting, 46–48
meetings
  communication rules in, 138–139
  framing as opportunities, 203
  global teams and, 134–137
  multiteaming and, 119–120
mental health, 210
mental models, 227–228
mentoring, 60–61
Michaels, Lorne, 76
micromanagement, 52
  delegating vs., 75–79
  multiteaming and, 127
Microsoft, 67–71, 174, 210
milestones, minor, 41–42
Milkman, Katy, 163
mindset, 217, 222
  of experimentation, 79
  growth, 68–69
  at Microsoft, 68
  set-up-to-fail syndrome and, 103
mission
  coaching and, 65–67
  working climate and, 6–8
modeling
  coaching and, 67–69
  communication in global teams, 144
  perspective-taking, 149–150
Moesta, Bob, 157–180
mood, 38
morale
  affiliative leadership and, 15–16
  democratic leadership and, 17
  leadership styles and, 24–25
Morley, David, 65
Mortensen, Mark, 109–128
motivation
  coaching and, 64–66
  coercive leadership and, 9
  for job changes, 160–163
  job switches and, 169
  micromanagement and, 90–91
  minor milestones and, 41–42
  multiteaming and, 121, 123
  power of progress and, 38–41
  power of small wins and, 33–54
  progress and, 36
  set-up-to-fail syndrome and, 83, 85, 91–93
multiteaming, 109–128
  costs of, 113–115
  managing the challenges of, 115–127
  prevalence of, 111–113
  preventing shocks in, 126–127
  pros and cons of, 110
  skill mapping and, 117–119

Nadella, Satya, 67–69
Neeley, Tsedal, 129–145

neocortex, 29–30
Netflix, 181
networks, managing, 229–230, 233
New York Yankees, 15
noncompliance, 92–93
nondirective coaching, 62, 63, 67
nonverbal communication, 139–140
nourishers, 38–41, 46–48

O.C. Tanner, 210
O'Neill, Paul, 15
"One More Time: How Do You Motivate Employees?" (Herzberg), 36
openness, 116–117
options, coaching and, 65
organizational structure, 218–219, 221
outcomes, excellence as, 192–193
out-groups, 88–90
ownership, 44, 204–205

pacesetting leaders, 3, 11, 18–20, 28–29
Penn, Andy, 218
PepsiCo, 43
perceptions
  global teams and, 139–142
  motivation and, 40–41
  set-up-to-fail syndrome and, 81–108
performance
  blame game and, 153–154
  continuous learning and, 223–237
  emotional intelligence, leadership, and, 3–8
  inner work life and, 35–38
  leadership styles and, 8
  management vs. development, 217–218
  progress loop and, 54–55
  psychological safety and, 199–206

set-up-to-fail syndrome and, 81–108
  theory of excellence and, 184, 190–192
performance appraisals, 71–73
perspectives
  framing as source of value, 202–203
  multiteaming and, 113–114
  team conflict and, 149–150
Peterson, Randall S., 147–155
politics, 230–231
power
  network management and, 229–230, 233
  structure and perception of in teams, 131–134
praise, 194
prep, do, review approach, 237–239
pressure, motivation and, 37–38
priorities
  multiteaming and, 119, 123–127
  recognizing feedback and, 195–196
  team leader, 115–123
process reengineering, 210–211, 215–218
productivity, inner work life and, 37–38. *See also* performance
professional development, 178–179
  coaching leadership style and, 22–23
  expertise and, 55–56
  job switches for, 163, 165–171
  for managers, 235–237
  managers and, 223–237
  prep, do, review approach to, 237–239
  your responsibility for, 223–228
progress
  daily checklist for, 49–51
  employee retention and, 158
  HR involvement in, 166, 176–179
  meaningful work and, 42–45

progress (*continued*)
    minor milestones and, 41–42
    power of small wins and, 33–54
    quests for in job switches, 163–166
    supporting, 46–48
progress loop, 54–55
progress principle, 34, 38–41
psychological safety, 199–206
    bridging boundaries and, 204–205
    evidence on, 201–203
    framing and, 202–203
    inquiry and, 203–204
Puget Sound Naval Shipyard, 170
pull factors, in job switches, 161–163
purpose
    coaching and, 65–67
    team management and, 231
    working climate and, 6–8
push factors, in job switches, 161–163
Pygmalion effect, 82

questions and questioning, 59
    coaching and, 62–63, 66
    employee interviews and, 168
    in global teams, 140–141
    psychological safety and, 204
quests for progress, 163–166

random error, 185
reality, coaching and, 64–65
recognition, 36, 193
reflected knowledge, 135
relationship building, 27, 30
    company politics and, 230–231
    in global teams, 130–145
    self-management and, 228–229
    team conflict and, 150–152
    in teams, 115–117
reputation, set-up-to-fail syndrome and, 93

resistance, set-up-to-fail syndrome and, 92–93
resources
    multiteaming and, 110, 112
    politics around, 230–231
respect, democratic leadership and, 17
responsibility
    pacesetting leadership and, 19
    working climate and, 6–8
retention, 157–180
    cost of attrition and, 159–160
    employee interviews and, 165, 166–171
    forces behind job moves and, 160–163
    HR and, 176–179
    managers and, 210
    quests for progress and, 163–167
    shadow job descriptions and, 165–166, 171–176
    traditional approaches to, 157–158
rewards systems
    affiliative leadership and, 14
    coercive leadership and, 9
    pacesetting leadership and, 19
    progress loop and, 54–55
    recognizing excellence and, 192–193
risk
    affiliative leadership and, 14
    multiteaming and, 123–125
Roberts, Gene, 77
Robertson, Julian, 75–76
Rometty, Ginni, 215

safety, psychological, 199–206
Sanders, Bill, 76
scapegoating, 149
Scoular, Anne, 55–73
Sculley, John, 43

self-awareness, 4
  of management ability, 223–228, 232, 234
self-confidence
  delegation and, 76
  nonverbal communication and, 139–140
  set-up-to-fail syndrome and, 82–83
self-management, 4, 228–229
set-up-to-fail syndrome, 81–108
  breaking out of, 95–96
  case studies on, 86–87
  challenges to changing, 101–104
  cost/benefit calculation and, 104–106
  cost of, 93–95
  deconstruction of, 87–93
  how it happens, 84–85
  in-group/out-group dynamics in, 88–90
  micromanagement in, 90–91
  preventing, 106–107
  research on, 87
  solving the problem of, 96–101
  subordinates' assumptions in, 91–93
  vicious circle in, 85–86
Shah, Priti Pradhan, 147–155
shutting down, 91–93
situational coaching, 62, 63–64
skills, building new management at scale, 213–215
skills mapping, 117–119
Soady, Cassie, 179
social awareness, 5
social distance, 130–145
  empathy and, 134–137
  power structure and perception and, 131–134
social skills, 5
solo dissenters, 148–150
SparcStart, 172
SPLIT framework, 130–145

Standard Chartered, 213–215, 221–222
standards
  pacesetting leadership and, 19
  working climate and, 6–8
Star Wars, 78
Stephens, Mark, 176
strengths, feedback on, 188–190
stress, from multiteaming, 113–115
Stringer, Richard, 6–8
success, mental model of, 227–228
systematic error, 185–187
systems, management models and, 215–218

talent marketplaces, 178
task conflict, 151–152
Taylor, Frederick, 171–172
teams and teamwork
  conflict management in, 147–155
  empathy in, 134–137
  global, effective, 129–145
  identity in, 121, 132–134, 139–142
  kickoffs for, 117
  language differences in, 135, 136, 137–139
  managing, 231–233
  overcommitted, 109–128
  perception mismatch in, 139–142
  power structure in, 131–134
  priorities for leaders of, 115–123
  psychological safety for, 199–206
  set-up-to-fail syndrome and, 93–94
  skills mapping in, 117–119
  technology and, 142–144
technology
  global teams and, 142–144
  management models in, 213, 215–218
  multiteaming and, 112, 120
  telecommunications, management models in, 213, 218–221

teleconferencing, 142–143
Telstra, 218–221
theory of excellence, 184, 190–192
theory of learning, 183, 187–190
theory of the source of truth, 182–183
time and time management
   in teams, 119–120
   unstructured time and, 135, 137
Torre, Joe, 15
toxins, 39–41, 46
transparency, in feedback, 181, 197–198
trust
   affiliative leadership and, 14, 15–16
   delegating and, 75–79
   in global teams, 135, 137
   global teams and, 129–130
   influence and, 229
   set-up-to-fail syndrome and, 82–83
   in teams, 115–117
truth, theory of the source of, 182–183, 184–187

underperformers, set-up-to-fail syndrome and, 81–108

values, working climate and, 6–8
videoconferencing, 142–143
vision, authoritative leadership and, 11
vulnerability, 117

warring factions, 152–153
Watson, James, 33–34
"What's Your Language Strategy?" (Neeley and Kaplan), 137–138
Whitmore, John, 59, 64
will, coaching and, 65–65
Winfrey, Oprah, 75
wins
   meaningful work and, 42–45
   model managers and, 48–54
   power of small, 33–54
work design, 178–179
work life
   employee retention and, 158
   performance and inner, 35–41

Zappos, 177

Work is hard. Let us help.

Engage with HBR content the way you want, on any device.

Whether you run an organization, a team, or you're trying to change the trajectory of your own career, let *Harvard Business Review* be your guide. Level up your leadership skills by subscribing to HBR.

HBR is more than just a magazine—it's access to a world of business insights through articles, videos, audio content, charts, ebooks, case studies, and more.

SUBSCRIBE TODAY
hbr.org/subscriptions